Mother Om

Om.
The universal sound of creation and peace.

Namaste

BY LEONIE PERCY

For my yoga practice

For my family

For all the mothers and children

I have the honour of teaching

And for Lael

My son

He is my inspiration and my greatest teacher

Love and light

Leonie

Published by Leonie Percy
Randwick, Sydney 2031

First published 2014

© Leonie Percy 2014

Editor: Lucy Tumanow-West

Graphic Design: Pauline Armour, Grafica

Illustrations: Neal J Thompson

Printed in Australia by Bright Print Group, Sydney

National Library of Australia Cataloguing-in-Publication entry

Author: Percy, Leonie, author.

Title: Mother Om : Connect with yourself and your child in one
                 mindful moment a day / Leonie Percy.

ISBN: 9780992475703 (paperback)

Subjects: Motherhood-Psychological aspects.
                 Stress (Psychology)-Prevention.
                 Yoga-Therapeutic use.
                 Meditation-Therapeutic use.
                 Mindfulness-based cognitive therapy.
                 Mind and body therapies.

Dewey Number: 306.8743

About the Author

Leonie is a loving mother, author and founder of Yoga Mamata.

After her marriage suddenly ended leaving her a single mother, she turned to her yoga practice for guidance. Leonie has been practising Hatha yoga for over 15 years. This path took her on a life-changing journey, buying her first business YogaBugs in 2010 in Sydney's east and becoming a qualified yoga teacher in 2011. Leonie was awarded Franchisee of the Year in 2012. Since then, she has studied yoga, psychology, meditation and mindfulness.

As a single mother, Leonie struggled with motherhood. In 2012 she combined her passion to keep families connected with her degree majoring in psychology to create Yoga Mamata.

Yoga Mamata offers yoga and mindfulness programs, clothing, nutritional cleansing and retreats for mums, kids and families. Its mission is to create a connected, compassionate community of like-minded families who are committed to making a difference in this overstimulated world.

Leonie has been interviewed for Studio Bambini and on The Carousel. She has also written articles for The Parenting Files and Bondi Beauty.

Leonie wrote her book *Mother Om – Connect with yourself and your child in one mindful moment a day* to motivate, inspire and empower other mothers who find motherhood stressful. Written from her heart, Leonie shares meditations and mindful tips on how to be a connected, contented and calm mother.

www.yogamamata.com

CONTENTS

INTRODUCTION

i am divine

Certain moments in life define us as individuals. I will never forget the moment my perfect husband and the father of my child told me he didn't love me anymore. I couldn't breathe and my whole world literally stopped. It was a complete shock. My heart was shattered. Our marriage ended in a heartbeat.

It was Christmas Eve, eight years since the day we met and our son, Lael, was about to turn two.

My husband and I had been so happy and in love. We'd travelled the world together and had often been described as the perfect couple. But somehow our connection had been broken, our relationship had died and I was devastated to be a single mother at the age of thirty-five.

This was not in my life plan, but I now know it was meant to happen on my life path.

The following year was full of sorrow as I learned to deal with the loss of this once-beautiful union.

To make things worse I had to go back to work in the corporate world. I have worked in sales since I was 12 years old, starting off door-knocking for Greenpeace, going on to sell millions of dollars in advertising sales for brands like Yellow Pages and Google. Now it just felt like all I was doing was making the world a more materialistic place.

On top of trying to deal with the emotional trauma, there was a new place to live, me working full-time, Lael going to childcare five days a week, new routines, parenting alone... it was all too much. Intense grief just poured out of me. At work I would cry uncontrollably, running to the bathroom to re-apply my makeup several times a day. At home I had to battle the night-time routine, dealing with an overtired toddler on my own. I could feel the stress manifesting itself in my aching body and distressed mind.

I could not live like this – I had to change my life.

The only thing that helped was my weekly power yoga practice. I would sweat out the avalanche of stress and each practice gave me a sense of calm – a sense that everything would be okay. And I would think about my own childhood, and my life up until now.

All I knew was that I loved yoga and my son.

When I was a child, I wanted to be famous so I could change the world.

I grew up in a seaside town in the UK and my childhood memories are happy ones. My wonderful parents have been together for over 40 years and my brother and sister are still very dear to me.

I was a rebellious teenager who sailed through school and graduated with an Honours degree majoring in psychology and communication studies at university. I then spent 10 years travelling the world, collecting magical moments in over 50 countries, all before I was 30. I loved travelling – I still do – but I did not know what my life purpose was.

I thought falling in love, being married and having a family would complete me. It didn't. But I had never once thought that being a divorced, single mother would become my reality.

However, I now know it was meant to happen so I could truly discover my dharma – my life path.

I truly believe I was born to be a spiritual teacher. My purpose in life is to teach yoga to children, mothers and families.

Yoga is my rock. I have been practising many different styles for over 15 years – Hatha, Iyengar, Ashtanga, Power Vinyasa, Kundalini, and Acro-yoga. My yoga journey has taken me on retreats to Thailand, India, Bali, Hawaii, Australia and New Zealand.

I was kicked out of my first yoga class for being disruptive – my sister and I were bending over, gases were released, and we started laughing hysterically. So it wasn't until my sore back, from my wild backpacking days, started yelling at me to go and do some stretching, that I realised the value and importance of yoga.

I enjoyed the physical release of built-up tensions in my body but soon discovered there is so much more to this ancient art than just stretching.

It gives me a mental break. There is no phone, no agenda, no child, no responsibility – just me and my breath.

The difference in the way I feel before and after practising yoga is profound: scattered, overwhelmed and exhausted turns into grounded, calm and energised.

Yoga genuinely helped me deal with the sudden breakdown of my marriage. Every time I practised yoga I cried; I let go of the pain and my broken heart healed just a tiny bit. The more yoga I did, the better I felt, and I have committed to follow this path that has changed my life forever.

Like many others, I came to yoga to benefit physically but have stayed to connect with it spiritually.

While I was pregnant I did a weekly class to help connect with my growing baby and prepare me for the birth.

After Lael was born my weekly yoga practice became a way of coping with the challenges of being a new parent.

I can also thank my grandfather for this awakening. Everyone says I am so like him. He was a deeply spiritual man who devoted his whole life, travelling the world inspiring and helping others, spreading the message of the Gospel.

When he died at 96 there were hundreds of people at his funeral paying tribute to his inspirational life. This made me ask myself what I had done to make a difference in this world. I didn't know then that my marriage would suddenly end a few months later and my spiritual journey would take flight.

Until that moment, I hadn't truly discovered just how powerful yoga can be and even though I had wanted to be a yoga teacher for a long time, fear had held me back.

In October 2010, at a yoga festival, I found YogaBugs – a franchised exercise program for children using a unique combination of yoga-inspired moves and imagination – I had a 'light bulb' moment and bought my first business.

The following year I qualified as a yoga instructor, which involved an intense 200-hour program of teacher training. Since then, I have studied yoga and psychology, meditation and mindfulness.

My journey with children's yoga took me on a magical adventure. I became a national trainer for YogaBugs and completed Family yoga training with Rainbow Kids and Radiant Child, which is Kundalini yoga for children.

My love of teaching kids, my passion to help mothers reconnect with themselves and my mission to keep families together led me to create Yoga Mamata.

Mamata, pronounced Maa-MAA-Taa, has its origins in the Sanskrit language and means 'mother's love'.

So here I am, on my constantly evolving path, having created Yoga Mamata and written *Mother Om*.

Much of the inspiration for this book came through the daily meditation practice that I found through yoga. I wanted to share the awareness I have gained – about how we can live our daily life as a mindfulness meditation, see each moment as a gift and expand our conscious mind to become great role models for our children. I believe this kind of conscious parenting can help us deal with the extremely stressful situations we encounter daily in motherhood.

Mother Om also comes from my belief that together we can create a society that values compassion, connection and community – but we need to be committed to a spiritual path to make that change.

So this book contains practical advice on how to take the first steps along a spiritual path. It includes calming tips, meditations and mindfulness practices for mothers, children and families, and shows how ancient teachings can have a profound impact on not just your life, but also the lives of your children.

Each chapter includes a Mamata moment (a tip or exercise to help you connect with yourself and your children) and ends with a reflection – a story that illustrates the learning and thoughts of that chapter.

Many of these stories come from where my yoga practice and teachings have met with my experience as a mother. Lael is now five years old and I confess I am not a naturally calm parent. In fact, without my daily practice I would not be able to cope with the demands of running a business and being a single mother.

The mother I write about in this book is the mother I aspire to be – one filled with unconditional love, compassion and grace – because as well as being incredibly rewarding, motherhood is a journey that is filled with guilt and frustration and we need to learn to let this guilt go and accept that all we can do is our best.

Single parenting is particularly stressful (sadly, over 40 per cent of marriages in Australia end in divorce) for both parents and children, and *Mother Om* holds much guidance for families in this situation. Yoga is a particularly good practice for mothers whose life path has taken them here, because it teaches us gratitude, forgiveness, how to let go of the past and move on from our situation. It teaches us how to be in control of our thoughts, feelings and perceptions and how to create the world we want. Yoga allows us to practise patience, compassion and tolerance, which is the ultimate path to long-lasting happiness.

This book demonstrates how, as mothers, we can find moments in our day that will create and restore a sense of calm. The meditations and Mamata moments can be practised alone, together as a family or with your children.

My hope is to empower, motivate and guide you so that you may find more connection with yourself, your child and the world around you.

Explore this book and use it as a guide. My intention is that you keep it close by, such as on your bedside table, and dip into it when you need to. Make a cup of tea mindfully and take a well-deserved break while reflecting on a chapter or two.

I have written this book from my heart in the hope that these words connect to your heart and your light within.

Together we can change our world and elevate ourselves above the challenges of motherhood, so we can become mothers who radiate compassion and grace.

We will become an inspiration to all who encounter our wisdom and we will shine brightly, guiding all who surround us home, like a lighthouse.

Enjoy this book. Enjoy your children. Enjoy yourself.

Leonie and Lael, Sydney, May 2014

The antidote to anger is compassion and the antidote to anxiety is peace.

TIME TO REFLECT

My journey has taught me that all we need is already right here in this present moment. Life is about what is happening now. We need to stop striving and start being.

Take some time to reflect on your own journey.

NOTES

_____

_____

_____

_____

_____

_____

_____

_____

_____

_____

_____

_____

_____

_____

_____

_____

_____

_____

_____

Find your mindful moment today

- Create a family gratitude jar by writing down what you are grateful for each day.

- Associate this moment in your day to becoming present.

- Spend some quality family time together.

- Tell your child and partner, if you have one, that you love them deeply.

- Book that holiday you have always wanted to take.

CHAPTER ONE
MAMATA YOGA

i am kind

YOGA MEETS MOTHERHOOD

The ancient practice of yoga gives us the tools to manage the emotional journey of motherhood. It can help us transform our mind to find a sense of balance and relief from the daily pressures of work, family and play.

Motherhood is a rollercoaster ride that lasts a lifetime. We all want to be the best mother we can be. We all want our children to thrive, feel loved and develop into secure, confident and resilient adults.

Motherhood brings happiness and joy but also frustration and exhaustion. Raising a child is a life-changing and spiritual experience. We realise the world does not revolve just around us and by awakening our conscious mind, we discover we are all connected.

Children make us see the world differently and they inspire us to want to change it.

Yoga, meanwhile, means the union of our body, mind and spirit, which are one. Yoga guides us to become our best self. It teaches us how to master our busy minds which clutter our doorways to bliss and freedom. Poses are linked to our breath. If yoga is not done mindfully, then it is just exercise.

A misconception about yoga is that is it just a physical practice of poses. We think we can only practise yoga by going to a yoga class but that is just the first step on our spiritual path.

Our breath is the bridge that connects us to all living things.

The principles of yoga are about being compassionate and kind to ourselves and others. We learn to take the time for self-care and to be truthful and content. We find the ability to let go of negativity, express gratitude and live in the present moment. It is about the connection between the teacher and the student, just like a mother and child.

How does yoga make us better mothers?

Yoga helps us become more aware of our thoughts and feelings, more present and more content.

Communication is compassion

We become more compassionate mothers through practising yoga. Realising our children are reflections of who we are and that they have feelings and want happiness too, we can see them as superior and practise humility.

By learning how to be present and spend quality time with your children, we will feel more content with motherhood.

We mother our children from our heads and hearts muddled up with advice from books and blogs. Yoga teaches us to mother our children from a place of love, not a place of fear. We mother from our own unconscious conditioning which we have inherited from our own childhood – which can be difficult if our own experiences as a child were not happy ones. We parent how we were parented. If we were shouted at or smacked as a child, then we may unconsciously shout or smack our children. This can be a very hard cycle to break. But yoga can help us change this because it teaches us to be compassionate in the way we communicate to our children.

Less guilt, more joy

Yoga teaches us to be kind to ourselves and to let go of some of the guilt that so often comes with being a mother.

The busy-ness of life means we are at risk of missing our children's childhood. So unplug and switch off from the many external demands, distractions and devices and tune into their world.

Inhale their loveliness. Yoga teaches us to play so we are able to relate to our child's world.

Learning to mother in the moment

Yoga teaches us to slow down and pause so we can regenerate from the challenges that motherhood brings.

When we slow down and become present and more aware of what is happening in each moment, we can guide and nurture our children through life, helping them to grow physically, mentally and emotionally – allowing and helping them to become their own person, not who we want them to be.

Softening within yourself

Children are not in control of their feelings. When we are stressed, our children absorb this, which makes it harder for them to cope with stress themselves.

When we relax and soften within ourselves, we are also soothing our children.

When we learn self-acceptance and self-compassion, we can teach our children to accept their own individuality.

Cultivating confidence, resilience and strength

Show your children how to get their confidence from within rather than responding to external factors. This promotes emotional resilience and teaches them that they cannot avoid the struggles life will bring, but they can deal with them in a healthy way.

A physical practice keeps our bodies fit and strong, which teaches our children that it is important to look after themselves too.

Yoga builds strength and balance so we are strong on the inside and relaxed on the outside. This allows us to manage and reduce stress.

Holding a challenging yoga pose teaches us that difficult moments do not last; that they will pass. We will have bad days and sleepless nights, but it is temporary. Some days we are balanced and other days we stumble. Each day is different and unpredictable and this is okay.

Recognising our imperfections

None of us are perfect mothers, but as long as we are present with our children, that is enough.

Use compassion and empathy to parent your children. Just as you may struggle with motherhood, recognise that childhood is no easy ride either.

In the developed world, many mothers work full-time and kids spend long hours in childcare, school and vacation care. Recognise the stress inherent in this and look to yoga to help you be present and calm with your children in the time you have together. Make it the best it can be.

Our job is to be their guiding light.

Manage your stress and be that guiding light

It is futile to be telling a child to calm down constantly if their most important role models are not demonstrating how to be calm.

As mothers, we need to learn how to manage our own stress so it does not affect our children. But suppressing our feelings is not the answer, just as dismissing our child's feelings is not.

If we are not engaging with our children and we are regularly dismissing their feelings, over time they, in turn, will learn to suppress their feelings. And this will inevitably lead to our children becoming the person they think they need to be to please us, not who they really are – which can, of course, lead to significant psychological issues in their adult life.

Yoga can help us achieve the openness and honesty needed here.When we shout, we should say sorry and explain that it is okay to get angry and that it is all part of being human.

Learn and teach empathy

Teaching our children empathy is an important part of being a mother. Empathy comes from a place of knowing from our own experience and understanding of how the other person is feeling. Kids need to learn about their feelings in everyday life. Discuss with your child the names of feelings and talk openly about them. What does angry feel like? How does it feel when this (situation) happens to you?

Children need to be taught the language of feelings. Research shows that if a child is not taught empathy, they will not have the ability to sustain good relationships with others.

Lead the way for your child by planting the seeds of empathy. Show them empathy in all of your thoughts and relationships, especially with them.

Yoga is not a destination; it is a journey, just like motherhood.

FINDING YOUR SPIRITUAL PATH

Being a mother and being on a spiritual path is the same. We can read all the books about motherhood or spirituality but we only learn and grow through our experience of it.

Yoga Mamata means mother's love and a mother's love is the heart of the family.

Our mission is to keep families connected and to help mothers, children and families feel content and calm in their daily lives.

This is why we have created unique workshops, programs and retreats. Mothers can do classes with their baby or their child, or with their entire family.

We are passionate about creating a connected, compassionate community of like-minded families who are committed to making a difference in this overstimulated world.

The Mamata philosophy

- Mothers learn to be compassionate and calm.
- Children learn resilience, reflection and empathy.
- Families share moments and stay connected.

☻ Mamata mindful moment

Whisper into your child's ear when they are sleeping that they are loved. This message goes to their higher self and makes them feel secure and loved.

The moment will also melt your heart because, being so distracted with life, you often forget to tell them this during the day.

....

MY REFLECTIONS

Yoga Mamata is the joy of my soul.

I wake up with gratitude every day and feel blessed to be able to share the gift of yoga with mothers, children and families. Yoga Mamata has been built on these values.

- ☻ Our core value is love. Self-love, mother's love, infinite love.
- ☻ Connection allows us to feel grounded, balanced, energetic, intuitive, grateful and resilient.
- ☻ Compassion is kindness, honesty and truth. We are whole-hearted and have great relationships.
- ☻ Commitment brings us clarity, experience, health, passion, authenticity and wisdom.
- ☻ Community brings us friendship and a sense of worthiness and belonging.

Find your mindful moment today

- Write down what motherhood means to you.

- Tell yourself every day : I am a loving mother.

- Go and try out a local yoga class with a friend.

- Understand being a mother is your yoga practice.

- Remember, compassion is communication.

CHAPTER TWO

THE PRINCIPLES OF YOGA

i am truth

> *Yoga is body-affirmative, powerful, peace-loving, ethical and practical. It helps us refine our inner state, which in turn creates our outer environment. It changes our chemistry and consequently, our destiny.*
>
> Natalia Perera, New York Spirit, Summer 2012

Dating back almost 5000 years, the principles of yoga are stated in the sutras – the 'threads' – by Patanjali. They outline the art and science of yoga for self-realisation.

In these ancient writings, yoga is described as being based on eight limbs or branches, like a tree, and on whichever branch we start our journey, we will be drawn to the other branches, as each is essential for our growth on this journey.

For example, we may be drawn to meditation before we start a physical practice, or vice versa.

We start with the first two limbs – the Yamas and Niyamas – here because of their particular relevance to mothers and children in the context of Mamata Yoga, but you can find plenty of discussion about the entire eight limbs elsewhere (go to the Yoga Sutras of Patanjali by Sri Swami Satchidananda for a good start).

We must teach our children kindness, or they will be taught violence.

YAMA PRINCIPLES

A Yama principle outlines our relationship with other people. Each is listed below with an example of how we can apply them in our life as mothers and how we can teach them to our children.

Ahimsa – non-violence and kindness

The blueprint for ethical living is to be compassionate to all living things.

We can practise Ahimsa in our physical yoga practice by listening to our body and being non-competitive. Our levels of loving-kindness, compassion and empathy are not determined by the number of difficult poses we can do. Ahimsa is spreading random acts of kindness and being non-violent in the way we talk to ourselves.

Let go of the guilt and frustration of motherhood. We have to be willing to make mistakes on every level and then be able to forgive ourselves over and over again.

Non-violence also means that children don't hit, kick or attack their friends or siblings.

Ghandi practised Ahimsa and changed a nation.

Satya – commitment to the truth

We have to be truthful and ethical in the way we deal with others. This means speaking our truth within ourselves and to our children.

We need to tell our children the truth about the world. Praise them in a meaningful way. Tell them they are great and full of goodness but don't tell them they are always 'good' or 'clever'. This will not make them resilient and it is not the truth.

Our children need to be able to reflect on the importance of telling the truth and being true to themselves

Asteya – non-stealing

We must not take what is not ours.

Be self-sufficient and do not rely on others for your own personal happiness. Be independent and less demanding of others.

We can teach our children to focus on what they need rather than what they want. Teach them to feel gratitude. This is not just wanting other kids' toys but also not taking attention away from others.

Brahmacharya – non-lust

We need to learn self-control and discipline.

By restraining ourselves from what we know will hurt us, like a relationship that makes us feel worthless, gives us inner strength.

Children will understand this when we teach them to manage their own emotions, and by providing them with simple routines to follow, like getting dressed, brushing teeth or making their lunch.

Aparigraha – non-greed

We can live a simple life and only take what we need.

We don't need unnecessary things and our children do not need to be constantly showered with gifts. They just need our time.
Only keep and want what you need.

NIYAMA PRINCIPLES

A Niyama principle outlines our relationship with ourselves.

Shaucha – purity

We can eat food that nourishes our body and live in a decluttered home.

Give away what we do not need to charity.

We can teach our children to clean up after themselves and that it is important to eat a healthy diet.

Santosha – contentment

We can find peace in whatever situation we are facing.

Be grateful and do not long for your situation to be different.

We need not worry about the past – it cannot be changed – and the future has not even happened yet.

Teach your children what you have is already enough and you do not need more to feel content. Teach them to enjoy the present moment.

Tapas – burning enthusiasm

Tapas is the fire in our belly that drives us.

Using this discipline allows us to direct our energy toward a life full of meaning and purpose.

We can teach children Tapas by getting them to do what is asked of them by using simple instructions.

Svadhyaya – self study

Life is challenging but we are in control of our actions.

Self-study helps us have better relationships, nourish our body and mind and learn from our weaknesses.

We can give our children choices and this will empower them to make their own decisions in life.

Reading books with positive affirmations and messages to our children will help them feel good about themselves. It is how they learn about their world.

Ishvara Pranidhana – surrendering the ego

Wherever we may be along our spiritual path, once we find our place, we surrender and commit ourselves to it fully.

We can teach our children that whatever path they choose, they need to embrace it with their own heart and live life in a wholehearted way.

We can encourage our children to try new things and to develop empathy by talking about other people's feelings.

The purpose of yoga is to bring change.

STEP ONE: THE BREATH

By just connecting to our breath with awareness, we are practising yoga.

We need to teach ourselves to breathe deeply.

You can tell a lot about a person by the way they breathe. When distressed, we take short, shallow breaths. When calm or in a deep sleep, we take rhythmic, deep breaths. When we meditate, our breath can be so quiet and soft, it is as if we are not even breathing.

Learning to breathe properly

On average, a person uses only a third of their lungs in their whole lifetime, yet we have the capacity to utilise this wonderful calming tool just by learning how to breathe effectively.

The breath is always with us. It is ours to use like it is our saving grace.

When we are feeling overstimulated and bombarded by pressure, we can deepen our breath and make our breathing slower and calmer.

Practise this by working on the quality of each breath you take, making it deeper, slower and steadier. Do this wherever you need to. This technique is very helpful during witching hour. Go into the bathroom, shut the door and take 10 deep, slow, steady breaths.

STEP TWO: THE BREATH AND THE YOGA CLASS

Our practice develops and our learning grows when we go to a yoga class. Our breath connects us to others as we flow and move together.

Yoga gives us profound inner strength.

Every time we back-bend, we lift our chest and ultimately our heart opens, allowing us to give and receive love.

Surrendering into a forward bend, we let go of worry, stress or anything that does not serve us, help us grow or make us happy.

🜪 *Mamata yoga moment*

When your child is upset, hug them and synchronise your breath with theirs. This will calm you both down and will help you feel connected to each other.

WHICH STYLE OF YOGA IS FOR YOU?

There are many different styles of yoga to choose from, all of which come from four main paths – Juana yoga for the intellect, the realisation of the truth; Bhakti yoga for the devoted; Karma yoga of action, the yoga of selfless service; and Raja yoga, the yoga of action, concentration or meditation.

Finding the connection is the most important part of the journey and even though a great yoga teacher has the power to transform your life, it is also a commitment that can only come from you.

The father of yoga, Krishnamacharya, believed yoga is about the connection between the student and the teacher, like that between a parent and child. His mission was to heal people through yoga and he tailored each class to each person's specific needs.

His most famous students were Jois, Iyengar and his son, TKV Desikachar, who each played a huge role in bringing yoga to the Western world. Together they developed Ashtanga Vinyasa yoga, which we know as the Sun Salutation. Vinyasa means flow, moving into each pose on an inhale or exhalation. This technique provides our culture, which seems mostly fixated on external factors, an opening to a path of internal connection and spirituality.

Yoga Mamata's philosophy is built upon the teachings of Krishnamacharya. Our core values are to create compassion, connection, community and commitment. These are incredibly important attributes for mothers, children and families.

For those who are new to yoga, try a few different classes and styles. You will find the connection that is right for you.

STEP THREE: LET YOGA TRANSFORM YOU

Through yoga, you discover who you are. It breaks you and then heals you.

Through yoga, you face your ego and learn to overcome your shadows – the unconscious, dark side of your psyche that consists of emotions like greed, anger, lust and selfishness. Everyone carries a shadow.

Yoga brings out your true personality – not the one you project to the world due to conformity or a need to be something you are not.

By finding courage when you face your fears, you stop striving and allow yourself to see the beauty of your shadows.

When you stop pretending, you start being. Pain starts to clear and your light starts to shine.

Once you stop striving, peace comes and it comes from within. You learn to honour your true self and communicate from a place of love, not fear.

The more you come from a place of love towards yourself and others, the more you will feel love.

WHAT YOGA IS...

- ❸ Yoga is non-competitive and does not judge.
- ❸ Yoga is for everyone and does not discriminate.
- ❸ Yoga is a practice you can use to realise your full potential.
- ❸ Yoga is a vehicle that helps you arrive in the present moment, freeing you from the pain of the past or the worry of the future.
- ❸ Yoga is not about making us better people but more of a process of removing barriers that prevent us from being connected to ourselves and others.

It is in life-changing moments like the birth of a child or the death of a marriage that these teachings reveal their most power.

WHAT YOGA TEACHES

We live in a culture that strives towards personal gain and materialistic values but yoga teaches us that the goal of happiness is through inner transformation.

Yoga teaches us to speak our truth and embrace our fears.

❸

You are already enough and you can become more resilient and take control of your emotional states.

Yoga teaches us that our individual thoughts and feelings matter and we can make the world a better place. Even a slight change can make a big difference. It connects us to Mother Earth and grounds us so we feel supported. This is why we practise yoga with bare feet.

WHAT YOGA CREATES AND ALLOWS

Yoga is a lifestyle and a spiritual philosophy with principles that can be used as a guide to live in a wholehearted and purposeful way.

Many of us have created barriers to protect ourselves from suffering but in doing this, we are stopping ourselves from feeling joy as well as pain. We cut ourselves off so we only feel a small amount of emotion.

By letting your guard down, you let life in, and the physical practice of yoga opens you up to the full range of human emotions. Certain postures challenge you as you hold them and breathe, allowing you to let go of built-up tension in your body.

Yoga allows release of mental trauma that has manifested in your physical body. It balances your energies and emotions.

If you embrace yoga, you will be content and want nothing more. You will learn to let go of fear and restraint. It connects your body, mind, spirit and loving heart.

Like music, yoga makes us feel.

☻ Mamata mindful moment

- Lie down and place one hand on your belly and the other on your heart. Breathe into your chest, then into your side ribs, then deep into your belly.

- Let your hands ride the wave of your breath.

- Breathe out from your belly, then your side ribs, and then exhale all the air from your chest.

- Repeat as many times as needed. This is a full yogic breath.

....

TIME TO REFLECT

The path to true happiness is an internal process and I have discovered not to rely on other people or external factors for my own happiness. We are the only ones who can make ourselves happy and through self-observation and a regular yoga practice, this can be achieved.

I live a Yogi lifestyle and follow the principles of being compassionate, honest and open. I am kind to myself and others. We each have a life path known as a dharma. If we choose to follow it our actions will result in a genuine kindness and truth.

I wear a charm on a necklace from a yoga retreat I went to in Thailand. It symbolises that when I practise yoga, I practise to Ganesh, the elephant-headed deity. In the yoga philosophy, elephants are the remover of all obstacles – or the barriers you create around yourself through your fears. I love elephants.

Find your mindful moment today

- Spread random acts of kindness.

- Speak your truth to yourself and others.

- Nourish your body.

- Go barefoot whenever you can.

- Start a journal and write down how you are feeling.

CHAPTER THREE

YOU NEED TO RELAX

i am zen

GOOD STRESS VERSUS BAD STRESS

We all need to relax. We were not made for the stress most of us create and endure. But if you want to do something about it, you need to understand what's going on in your brain when you are stressed and when you are relaxed.

Your brain has three key regions – the stem, the limbic region and the cortex – and dealing with stress is mainly the domain of the limbic system (also known as the 'emotional' or 'mammalian' brain because its evolution from our warm-blooded relatives marked the beginning of social cooperation in the animal kingdom).

When you perceive a threat – whether it's real or not – your limbic system automatically gets your nervous system into action, with hormones being released that set off metabolic reactions to help you cope with an emergency situation. This comes from what's called your sympathetic nervous system (it activates in sympathy with the danger you are feeling) and is known as the 'fight or flight' mechanism.

Your adrenal glands release adrenaline and other hormones that speed up your breathing and heart rate to get the oxygen-rich blood to your brain and muscles in a hurry so you can think quickly and run fast. They likewise stop the oxygenated blood going to any areas unnecessary for dealing with the emergency (such as growth, reproduction and the immune system).

So, in a life-threatening situation your mind and body go into a kind of temporary metabolic overdrive. Fight or flight can save your life, but freezing, or doing nothing, simply leaves the stress in your body.

The problem is that some of the stress hormones, such as adrenaline, don't stop when the stressful situation ends and their prolonged effect can be damaging to many of your body processes (including growth, reproduction and the immune system).

Also, many of us 'call on' these hormones continuously because we are frequently or constantly under stress – chronic stress – and the body produces the long-term stress hormone cortisol. One effect of this hormone on your body cells is that your metabolism slows down and your body stores fat. You can exercise every day, do yoga and eat organic food but when you are stressed and have cortisol in your body, it is very difficult to maintain good health.

A depressed immune system and high blood pressure are other effects of prolonged stress implicated in the development of such illnesses as chronic fatigue syndrome, Type-2 diabetes and asthma.

THE CHILL FACTOR

Sometimes, when the stress is always there, you do not even acknowledge it and soldier on with a stiff upper lip, regardless. Meanwhile, your mind fills itself with anxiety and worrying thoughts.

Perhaps this will sound familiar : You move house, change jobs, travel, have children, run a business, work 40 hours a week plus you deal with grief and loss. The stress builds and builds and you ignore the symptoms until your health fails and the ill effects cannot be ignored any longer.

To counteract the negative effects of stress, you need to stimulate your body's parasympathetic nervous system – the part that overcomes the fight and flight effects of the sympathetic nervous system – and bring on your body's relaxation response.

It is via messages from the limbic system of your brain that your body and mind can become calm and balanced again. So, if you are under constant stress in your life, you will need to send these calm messages regularly.

A simple solution

The simple act of deep breathing can have such a positive impact on your life with benefits for your nervous, digestive and reproductive systems and your general wellbeing.

Breathing from your belly stimulates your parasympathetic nervous system, which promotes rest and regeneration.

Deep breathing may only calm you for a short period, however. So if the threat causing your stress is the ongoing psychological kind, rather than the immediate physical type, you will need to change the habitual fight and flight reaction your sympathetic nervous system is constantly triggering.

Enter meditation and yoga

By using the repetition of meditation to observe and understand your behaviour patterns, you can create new ones.

Changing these deeper patterns can be a life-changing experience with long-lasting effects on the way you view yourself, others and the world around you.

In meditation, each time you focus the mind and deepen the breath you are taking a mental break and triggering your body's ability to rest and regenerate.

With practise, this mindfulness can build your mental muscles, allowing you to retrain your brain and handle situations differently, so that what once caused you stress will no longer bother you.

When you reduce the effects of stress, you can free yourself from suffering, and stop getting so lost in your own story. Instead of acting in a habitual way, you can start acting with more wisdom and grace. You can become more compassionate.

Yoga and mindfulness allow you to take a mental break from the daily stress that you create for yourself in your thoughts, words and actions.

Meditation is medication for our mind.

✪ Mamata relaxing moment

The best way to get in touch with how you are really feeling is to do a body scan.

- Lie on the floor or sit on a comfortable chair. Close your eyes.

- Scan each part of your body, starting with your toes and going right up to the crown of your head.

- Consciously tune in and feel each part. Notice comfort and any discomfort.

- Use the breath to breathe into each body part, releasing any tension.

....

TIME TO REFLECT

The structure and function of the human brain is complex with different parts taking longer than others to develop. For example, the cortex – which is involved in language and consciousness, where we process our experiences and where our memories are created through thought, sensation and reflection – takes the longest to develop. This is especially so for the front part – the pre-frontal cortex – which is responsible for thinking, planning and decision-making.

The largest part of the brain is the cerebrum, which is divided into right and left hemispheres. The left hemisphere is responsible for logical language-based thinking and helps us understand right from wrong. The right hemisphere controls our intense emotions, nonverbal communication and gives us our sense of self and others.
Children are typically right-brain thinkers, ruled by their emotions.

Because of this, until our children are around four years old and their left hemisphere development kicks in, we cannot expect them to think logically or be able to put feelings into words.

Reflect on this when you are feeling exasperated with your child for not listening to you and doing what you ask, and don't take it personally.

Also consider that our experiences will influence our brain's development. We will become skilful at whatever we practise.

Consider, too, that mindfulness helps us to balance the two sides of the brain. According to neuropsychiatrist and neurobiologist Daniel J Siegel of the Mind Sight Institute, the brain has two sets of circuits – one about the physical world and one about the world of the mind – both very different.

When we relate to others through empathy, Dr Siegel considers this to be called 'mind sight'; showing our interconnectedness. If we do not engage this connection in our brain, if we do not practise compassion, we shut down the skills we need to develop mind sight.

So, again, this is where mindfulness in meditation and yoga is so valuable, and from an early age. Reflection – developed in the middle pre-frontal cortex of the brain – keeps relationships strong and teaches us resilience. It connects the different activities of the brain, helping us to attune to others, and gives us empathy and insight.

We feel a sense of oneness.

Find your mindful moment today

- Write about what stress you are feeling in your journal.

- Notice how you are breathing
  - is it deep or shallow?

- Observe how you are sleeping
  - is it soundly or restlessly?

- Take some time to reflect on your situation.

- Cleanse your body every day to release toxins.

CHAPTER FOUR
MAMATA MINDFULNESS MEDITATION

i am mindful

> *A bird sitting in a tree is never afraid of the branch breaking because her trust is not on the branch, but on her own wings. Always believe in yourself.*
>
> Author Unknown

Mindfulness is living in the present moment. It is the art of paying attention to whatever we are doing, without any judgement.

The purpose of practising a mindfulness meditation is not to eliminate thoughts but just to notice them. This will reduce the impact they have on your emotional state.

It helps you to choose what you are paying attention to and how to relate to your experiences.

Mindfulness has been proven to assist with finding fulfilment and happiness. It allows you to reconnect when you have lost focus and relates to your five senses – sight, touch, sound, smell and taste. You can also focus on the sixth sense – your intuition and your thoughts and feelings.

Your children can be taught how to meditate and how to be mindful. These techniques give them coping skills to deal with the pressure of life in our society.

MAKE LIFE MINDFUL

With practise, you can turn little bits or your entire life into a mindfulness meditation. You can sit in stillness for several minutes a day, or simply be mindful while carrying out a daily ritual, like brushing your teeth.

Once you master this skill, you can turn any mundane chore into a wonderful mindfulness meditation experience. You can create triggers and reminders so you remember to practise this art.

With practise you can become more present with yourself and your children.

A daily yoga class is nothing more than a dream for most mothers, but you can find moments in your day to connect to who you truly are. These moments will leave you feeling energised and calm and will empower you as a mother to juggle the daily routine and be a great role model for your children.

MAKING CHILDREN MINDFUL

Children reflect their surroundings like a lake reflects a mountain. If we are solid and calm, they will be too. If we represent an erupting volcano, they will mirror this.

Relieve children of the pressure of being plugged into technology from an early age. With too much technology time, pressure from school, exhaustion from being overscheduled and little quality time with their parents, children often end up feeling anxious and ungrounded.

We can practise compassion as we parent our children. Teach them how to deal with anxiety and other unhelpful emotions using breathing techniques and meditations. Give them the skills to cope with life and to find stillness within.

Mindful meditation teaches children empathy, compassion and the art of reflection, which in turn enables them to have better relationships and to become resilient. It helps them to let go of overwhelming thoughts and feelings and come back into balance emotionally and spiritually.

Grounded, focused and calm children are confident children. They know who they are and they know their purpose and place in this world.

UNDERSTANDING MEDITATION

The best analogy I have come across about what meditation does for our minds is from Dr Christopher Willard's book *Child's Mind*. Imagine a blackboard or whiteboard. At the end of the day the board is quickly wiped but marks remain from what has been written and drawn there. But when the board gets cleaned properly with a cloth, all the marks are completely gone and the board is clean.

This process can also apply to your busy mind. Removing all the fragments of your daily thoughts cleans your mind to give you a fresh, clean board to work with each day.

Meditation helps you to understand and observe your thoughts.

You can choose if you want to indulge in your thought patterns – if you have a negative thought, you can simply just acknowledge it and think of something else.

Like clouds in a sky, thoughts come and go. They are temporary.

Meditation is actually quite easy to learn, but it can take a lifetime to master.

When you feel sad, you can take comfort that it will pass and it is okay to feel that way. It is part of being human, but it is temporary and we are always on an upward spiral.

So when things get tough it may feel like we have regressed, but we can comfort ourselves by knowing we are still climbing our spiral – and one day we may wake up and be enlightened.

Changing your thinking

If you have a negative thought, it is said you have nine seconds until you start to get stuck in that story and attract other thoughts of the same nature.

We can change "I am so tired... it is because I never get a break... I wish I had just five minutes to myself... but I don't have the time..." to "I am tired but I love being a mum" or "I am really tired so I am going to book myself a massage because I deserve it".

Training your mind

Facing your thoughts by allowing your mind to settle can be a daunting experience; being bombarded with the story of your life can be overwhelming.

Training your mind can be like trying to train a puppy – the more you try to restrain it, the more it jumps all over the place. But you can put the puppy on a leash. It will still try to run in many different directions, but with practise you can train your mind to 'sit'; to find stillness.

Look at the sky

All you need to do is to look at the sky. See how incredibly beautiful it is. Day or night, it is constantly changing, like your mind. Some days you feel grey and cloudy, other days are clear and you shine like a star. These feelings change from moment to moment. Just like your life can change in a heartbeat.

Learn to be present

Meditation shows you how to let go of your ego and be present in each moment. It gives you a break from the way you analyse and judge your life. That's why teaching children meditation can be easier than teaching adults – they don't judge and analyse; they are already living in the moment.

CHOOSING A MEDITATION STYLE

Like yoga, there are different types and styles of meditation. What may seem easy for some people will be more challenging for others.

Just as you may respond better to sounds rather than images, you may prefer a similar meditation technique. For some, listening to healing music allows the mind to become calm; others will prefer to focus on something visual, like a candle.

As you progress further along this path, you can start to focus on the silence between sounds or the space in between your thoughts. You can practise meditation sitting on a cushion or lying down. You can do a walking meditation, go for a run, surf, listen to music, dance, stomp, shake; do whatever helps clear your mind.

WHAT TO EXPECT IN MEDITATION

Your mind will wander. It is made to think. The trick is to let go of expectations – just observe and accept whatever arises in your mind.

The average person has about 70,000 thoughts a day, so in a 10-minute meditation you might experience 486 thoughts. Do not panic: this is normal.

You can distract your mind by focusing on your breath, or you can silently repeat a mantra.

As you inhale, you can mentally breathe in peace and as you exhale, you can breathe out calm. Or breathe in strength and breathe out negativity. Or simply focus on your belly: as your belly lifts, silently say "rising", and as it falls, silently say "falling".

JUST BE

One of the most difficult parts of meditation is to cultivate love and compassion towards yourself.

The mind is like a butterfly, flitting all over the place. If you believe in yourself, it can be tamed and with practise you will find stillness from moment to moment.

Just observe and allow whatever arises to just be; do not judge.

Do not try to stop the thoughts or expect a quick fix. Like learning to ride a bike, meditation takes practise, time and discipline. Don't quit.

Try for just a minute at first and then try for just a little longer each time.

You will not always experience a peaceful mind when you meditate. The trick is to just observe. See your thoughts float away in a bubble, or on a leaf in a stream, or in a balloon or resting on a cloud. Let them float away.

MY YOGA JOURNEY

My journey began with a 21-day meditation challenge, endorsed by Oprah Winfrey and Deepak Chopra. I had to meditate for 15 minutes a day and they emailed me each day with a guided meditation and mantra which established the habit of doing it daily.

Then I signed up for Mindful in May – a great organisation that raises money for clean drinking water in Rwanda – to commit to meditate every day for 31 days. Now I use an app on my phone.

I like to meditate about a person – known as a Metta meditation – which helps me to focus on sending loving-kindness to others and helps cultivate compassion. You can focus on your child, a friend or someone in need.

Imagine this person's presence and how they make you feel, and send them gratitude. It can also be done to someone who is challenging us.

There is an old adage that says:
40 days of practice to change a habit,
90 days to confirm the habit,
120 days, we are the habit and
1000 days, mastery of the new habit.

We need to practise a new skill to master it.

CREATE A SPACE

Set up a special place in your home for meditation. Add a cushion, a yoga mat, some flowers and a candle.

School-aged children will love doing this. For younger children, have a calm-down box and get them to put in things that make them feel still and good inside. Put it in a place where they can take a moment to control their reactions and feelings. And when you feel yourself getting angry, you can go and sit in the corner with the calm-down box to set a good example.

Places to try meditation

- In your car
- In a park
- On the bus
- On a plane
- In the bath
- On your lunch break
- At home, with your legs up against a wall
- In bed, as soon as you wake up

☻ Mamata meditation moment

- Light a scented candle and watch the flame.

- Gaze at the flame softly until your eyes start to water, then close them and picture the flame in your mind's eye. This stimulates intuition and focus.

- Another technique is to watch the candle until your eyes water and then lie down in relaxation. Let your child join you. They may wriggle around at first but they will calm down as they watch the flame dancing.

You can bring back some balance into your life.

☻

TIME TO REFLECT

At one stage of my life I was teaching yoga almost daily but I was not meditating. In fact, I put it off for so long that I became really stressed out and found myself getting impatient with my son all of the time.

Being a yoga teacher and not having a daily meditation practice is like a light without a light bulb.

I feel like being a parent is similar – we have to practise, make mistakes, try new things, be compassionate, grow, fail, learn, explore and see what works for us, as we are all unique individuals.

As a busy mum I find the car to be the perfect place to stop and be still. I play a CD or just focus on the sounds around me and breathe. Driving is also the time to practise Bhakti yoga, which is a path of devotional yoga. By chanting and absorbing the vibrations of listening to calm music and healing mantras, we remain connected to our chosen path. My son and I sing yoga songs on the way to school and when we are stuck in traffic.

Find your mindful moment today

- Look at the sky, observe the clouds, and liken them to your thoughts.

- Use the blackboard analogy as a daily reminder to clear your mind.

- Light a candle and practise a meditation.

- Find a part of your day that works for you to find stillness.

- Create a special peaceful space in your home.

CHAPTER FIVE
SPINNING WHEELS OF ENERGY

i am free

> *Chakras are like radars but they are also like sponges. Whatever is going on in our world, we absorb and radiate that energy.*
> Daphne Ravey, Psychologist, Shakti Bliss

Need more energy?

Yoga can give you the best kind of energy – the kind that comes from within.

Yoga actually works its magic on your mind, body and spirit via the seven main chakras. Known as spinning wheels of energy, the chakras are located in a straight line from the base of your spine to the crown of your head.

Energy flows through your body and is connected through the chakras in an energy channel called the sushmana nadi, which travels from your spine up into your brain.

CHAKRAS, NADIS AND ENERGIES

Nadis (pronounced "nah-dees") are energy centres in your body. Your body has two different energies that need to be balanced.

Ida is your feminine energy – the cool, calm energy on the left of your body – the parasympathetic nervous system. Pingala is your masculine and active energy and is produced on the right side of your body – the sympathetic nervous system.

If you need to get rid of a specific energy, you can simply block the opposite nostril. So to calm down or get to sleep, expel the hot air from your right nostril and to energise yourself, expel the cool air from your left nostril.

Yoga and chakras

During a yoga class, each set of poses is designed to stimulate a different chakra, and can be done in the order of how they sit within your emotional body, from the base of your spine to the crown of your head. Sometimes, a whole yoga class can be planned to balance just one chakra.

Yoga helps balance these energies and prepares the body for shavasana, known as the relaxation or corpse pose.

A matter of balance

Chakras move in and out of balance on a daily basis throughout a person's life. Yet each must be in balance for us to be in a state of harmony.

Yoga is a tool you can use to transform your body's energy centres. Your chakras influence your thoughts, moods and health and yoga allows you to elevate this energy up the chakras and change your consciousness.

After this happens, you will feel different, see life differently, and because you feel different, you will act differently. As a consequence, your attitude towards life changes, as well as your relationships with yourself and others, including your children.

This is how a yoga practice works to leave you feeling lighter.

About chakras

Each chakra has a colour and affects the way you feel. It can become overactive or deficient, but ideally you want them to be balanced. If you can regulate your energy flow, you can increase your levels of general wellbeing.

When a chakra is open, energy moves freely around the body. If one is blocked or unbalanced, you can become ill on a physical, emotional and spiritual level.

This energy is known as your life force, or prana.

The mind/body connection

The teachings we base this understanding upon come from the East, where the approach to healing the body sees the mind as part of the body and energy blockages as central to any problem.

We cannot see these energies. In the West there is a tendency to heal what is tangible and physically wrong within the body.

The Eastern belief is that the chakras spin as energy flows through the body, but the prana cannot flow when the chakras are blocked. An example could be when a child who is not shown any affection grows up having difficulty opening their heart chakra – representing love and compassion – to others. Or a child who was told to be seen and not heard may have a blocked throat chakra, which represents communication.

The seven main chakras

Each chakra has a colour, a meaning, a sense and an element associated with it.

Crown	Purple	Transcendence	Higher self	Thought
Brow	Indigo	Inspiration	Light	Intuition
Throat	Blue	Communication	Hearing	Ether
Heart	Green	Love	Touch	Air
Solar plexus	Yellow	Willpower	Sight	Fire
Sacral	Orange	Sexuality	Taste	Water
Root	Red	Survival	Smell	Earth

CHAKRAS IN DETAIL

The energy flows up the spine from the root to the crown, and each chakra must be unblocked for the energy to be able to move to the next.

Different chakra issues have different consequences. For example, if we expel all our energy through the lower chakras, then we have no more energy to clear the higher chakras. And because the different chakras have different key characteristics and roles, specific blockages will have specific outcomes.

Generally, the root, sacral and solar plexus chakras represent our personal and physical connection, while the heart, throat, brow and crown chakras represent our spiritual connection.

The quality of your energy,
is the quality of your life.

Root chakra

This chakra is at the base of your spine. To visualise it, imagine a spinning red wheel.

The root chakra represents survival – our need for food and shelter. It is linked to feeling safe and secure and when it is balanced, you feel grounded, comfortable and connected. When it is unbalanced, you may have low self-esteem and be prone to depression and addiction; you may also feel disconnected, be underweight, restless, disorganised and have no boundaries.

If you have too much root chakra energy you may feel greedy, lazy, overweight, rigid and controlling and be selfish and materialistic. You may also experience physical manifestations within your body such as constipation or other bowel issues and frequent illness.

In yoga, standing poses such as the warrior sequence connect and balance the root chakra to help you feel centred and grounded. We start a yoga class by either sitting or lying down so we feel our connection to the earth via the root chakra.

To help balance the root chakra

- Give yourself a foot massage
- Burn oils or light a scented candle to stimulate your sense of smell
- Buy flowers to bring colour and life to your surroundings
- Create a beautiful living space using the art of feng shui
- Add some red cushions to your home
- Wear a tiger's eye or fire agate crystal
- Go barefoot

Sacral chakra

Your sacral chakra is located in your lower abdomen. To visualise it, imagine a spinning orange wheel.

The sacral chakra represents your sexuality and your pleasures. It is the centre for your emotions and is connected to fertility.

When the sacral chakra is balanced, you feel open and in touch with your feelings – you are positive and trusting. When it is unbalanced, you feel guilt, self-pity and envy and you may have a fear of sex and be jealous and obsessive.

If you have too much sacral chakra energy, you might be addicted to sex or pleasure and be ruled by your emotions. Physical manifestations include fertility issues, menstrual issues and impotence.

In yoga, sequences of forward bends and hip openers help balance the sacral chakra. Hip openers and side stretches stimulate your kidneys and balance this chakra.

To help balance the sacral chakra

- Drink plenty of water or herbal tea
- Meditate in the bath
- Go dancing
- Wear an orange scarf
- Go for a swim or spend time near water
- Let go of unhealthy emotions
- Have a lymphatic drainage massage

Solar plexus chakra

Your solar plexus is located in your navel. To visualise it, imagine a spinning yellow wheel.

The solar plexus chakra aids the function of the digestive system and liver. It is also the power station where your drive, courage, confidence and will emanate from.

When the solar plexus chakra is balanced you will feel confident, disciplined and responsible, meet challenges, have good self-esteem and a great sense of humour.

When this chakra is unbalanced, you may have low energy, low self-esteem, poor digestion, blame others and be unreliable. Too much solar plexus chakra energy can make you an aggressive, dominant and controlling workaholic. Physical manifestations include stomach issues, chronic fatigue and diabetes.

In yoga, we twist the body and do a series of core exercises to release built-up toxins in the body, especially the liver. A strong core protects your lower back and creates stability for the front and back of our body and also gives you inner strength.

To help balance the solar plexus chakra

- Catch some rays – the sun governs this chakra
- Do a digestive cleanse, eat fibre and eat slowly
- Listen to that gut feeling – exercise your intuition
- Spend time alone
- Be a leader
- Buy a yellow handbag

Heart chakra

Your heart chakra is located in the centre of your body. To visualise it, imagine a spinning green wheel.

Your heart is the central chakra where heaven and earth meet. It represents love and compassion.

When your heart chakra is balanced you feel energised and are able to give and receive love. You are kind and peaceful.

When this chakra is unbalanced you may lack confidence and be withdrawn, feel isolated, lack empathy and be fearful of intimacy. You may also be narcissistic.

With too much heart chakra energy you may be clingy, over-emotional and demanding. Physical manifestations include stiff shoulders, asthma, immune deficiency and chest pains.

In yoga class there is a sequence of back bends and chest-opening poses that will open up your heart centre. Breathing exercises also balance this chakra, whose associated element is air.

To help balance the heart chakra

- Give someone you love a massage
- Laugh out loud
- Breathe deeply
- Hug your child
- Do a loving-kindness meditation
- Get a rose quartz crystal for compassion
- Have an aromatherapy massage

Throat chakra

Your throat chakra represents purity, truth and communication. Imagine a spinning blue wheel in your throat.

When your throat chakra is balanced you feel inspired and balanced; you say what you mean and find your inner voice and self-expression. You are patient and listen well.

When this chakra is unbalanced you may not speak up, you hold your breath, criticise and struggle to verbalise your feelings.

If you have too much throat chakra energy you will gossip, dominate, interrupt, talk too much and won't listen. Physical manifestations may include thyroid issues, acid reflux, unhealthy teeth and gums and ear infections. Toxins will build up if you do not speak your truth.

In yoga, we activate this chakra when we do a shoulder stand or lift our neck or back up in a pose. Reading philosophical texts, learning about cultures and exploring powerful ideas also opens and unblocks this chakra.

To help balance the throat chakra

- Have a facial
- Find your voice
- Sing or chant "Om"
- Practise the art of listening
- Listen to stories or classical music
- Wear blue eyeliner
- Express yourself

Brow chakra

Your brow chakra is situated in between your eyes. To visualise it, imagine a spinning indigo wheel.

The brow chakra relates to the way you visualise, perceive and think about your world.

When your brow chakra is balanced you are inspired, intuitive and have a vast imagination. You see beyond your physical nature and can see and create your future. This chakra creates inner harmony between your body, mind and spirit. You are honest. When this chakra is unbalanced, you have a poor memory, lack imagination and only do things one way.

When you have too much brow chakra energy you may have nightmares, become fixated on things and even have hallucinations. You can become self-absorbed and dysfunctional.

In yoga we use this powerful chakra throughout a class in focus, balance and concentration. Finding a focal point for your eyes to gaze upon helps you stay in the pose for longer. Lie on your back and grab your toes in happy baby pose to stimulate this chakra.

To help balance the brow chakra

- Be honest and open
- Get out of your comfort zone
- Spend time in nature
- Use positive affirmations
- Practise doing a handstand against a wall
- Go on a Yoga Mamata retreat
- Roll and exercise your eyes

Crown chakra

Your crown chakra is located on the top of your head. To visualise it, imagine a spinning purple wheel. In newborns this spot is the fontanelle.

Your crown chakra is your connection to the divine. It is said to be a thousand-petal lotus that shines above your head like a halo.

This chakra connects you to your belief systems; your ego is replaced with universal consciousness.

When the crown chakra is balanced you are intelligent, thoughtful, open-minded and spiritually connected. You experience fulfilment and peace and have innate wisdom. You connect with your life path and your life has meaning and purpose as you honour your true self.

When this chakra is unbalanced, your mind is closed and you lack meaning and purpose. You may have learning difficulties or a rigid belief system.

When you have too much crown chakra energy you are not connected to your heart and you can become fanatical. Physical manifestations include intense headaches, brain tumours, amnesia and dementia.

In yoga we use this chakra for contemplation and in meditation. It is our spirit.

To help balance the crown chakra

- Create a sacred space
- Practise visualisations
- Practise mindfulness
- Spend time reflecting

- Meditate
- Transform your mind – practise gratitude
- Choose love over fear

CHAKRA DEVELOPMENT IN CHILDREN

Between the ages of one and three years, children are developing the three base chakras – root, sacral and solar plexus. From four to seven years, the heart chakra develops. The throat chakra develops around the time children start speaking and again at seven to 12 years, then the brow chakra comes in from 12 to 21 years. Children have their crown chakra from birth.

The root chakra

The root chakra represents survival and safety. At this age, children are trying to find their feet, get grounded and navigate their bodies, which is a challenge.

Until around the age of two, a child does not have full control of their body movements. Imagine them in the spirit world, floating around, and then they are born into a body they do not know how to control. They get frustrated and of course cannot express themselves.

The sacral chakra

This chakra governs relationships and the sense of pleasure and this is when children start to relate to other people.

Around this time they also become toilet trained and fussy eating can develop as they are acquiring their sense of taste.

The solar plexus chakra

The power station of the chakras, the solar plexus, develops between 18 months and four years, along with a child's confidence – and their will and defiance, which are displayed through temper tantrums. All this is a healthy part of development as children become their own person and start to make their own decisions.

The heart chakra

Children need so much love and affection and they just need us to spend quality time with them as this chakra develops between the ages of four and seven.

The throat chakra

Children develop their throat chakra when they are learning to talk and also when speaking their truth becomes apparent from seven to 12 years old.

The brow chakra

Teenagers develop the brow chakra from 12 to 21 years old when their thoughts determine who they are; they develop their intuition.

The crown chakra

Children have their crown chakra from birth. It relates to the integration of a person's whole being – physical, mental, emotional and spiritual.

RECLAIMING YOUR ENERGY

Why do you always feel so exhausted? It could be that we run on energy that comes from the ground but because we are always wearing shoes, we may have lost our connection to the earth.

A great way to feel grounded is to simply remove your shoes.

Energy goes up into your chakras but an imbalance can occur at the sacral chakra level which deals with friends, lovers, children and addictions – in sustaining your relationships. As a mother you invest so much time and energy in your family and have little left for you.

Imagine the energy running up your spine along the chakras, flowing first into the root chakra at the base, then up to your sacral chakra. If all your energy is given away here, there is no energy left to go to the higher chakras – which means self-esteem issues, a closed heart, issues with communicating your truth, poor intuition and a life that lacks meaning and purpose.

Keep some energy for yourself

We expel our energy in our relationships thinking we need to do this to find a sense of worth in the world. We feel we need love to come from the outside. The more we send out our energy here, the more empty we feel. The emptier we feel, the more we seek from the outside. But the reality is this is not sustainable and will result in a breakdown.

You become co-dependent in your relationships with others by encouraging friends and family to rely on you all the time. The more you give your energy away, the more others will take. This is where yoga comes in to save you. It teaches you not to give everything away and to put in some boundaries.

Through yoga you become full of energy and show others how to become independent.

Your root and sacral chakra hold a lot of fear and guilt that comes up in relation to your world and relationships. But as a mother you must come from a place of love, not fear. You must learn to say "no" to get a sense of self-surrender. Take a pause.

Call on your chakras

You need a strong root chakra to feel safe to create these boundaries and to make changes in your world and face life's struggles; you need to develop a strong sense of love and compassion.

Your solar plexus is your ego and you need to have a strong sense of self to be able to say "no". Once you start to practise yoga, you start to make lifestyle changes and create these boundaries and your false ego – the one you project onto the world – starts to fade. Your solar plexus is awakened through your struggles; it makes you stronger and fearless, and when you say "no" to others, you develop a healthier ego.

Finally, once we soften, we awaken the heart chakra, where the ego melts and we have compassion for all.

✿ Mamata energy-restoring moment

A very quick way to calm yourself and reclaim some energy is to practise the Sitali breath, which expels hot air from the body. This is perfect to do in the car when you have been rushing around. This is also great for children to do.

Curl your tongue and inhale and exhale, or just place your tongue out of your mouth and breathe like a puppy.

MY REFLECTIONS

When my marriage broke down, it felt like all my chakra wheels stopped spinning. Part of me died.

I felt like my world had been pulled out from underneath me. All roots were gone. I lost my connection to everything, feeling abandoned and isolated and suffering from intense loneliness.
My root chakra was shattered.

My sacral chakra was in overdrive because I was needy, over-emotional, irrational and depressed. My solar plexus was blocked, causing me to lose all confidence and develop low self-esteem.

My heart chakra shut down.

The whole area around my heart was affected, including the muscles in my upper back, which almost became fused together with the stress.

My throat chakra was unbalanced because I couldn't speak my truth and I felt like I was suffocating, I couldn't breathe properly and I was having panic attacks.

However a tiny voice in my brow chakra – my intuition – told me that I would be okay, and each time I practised yoga I glimpsed rays of light shining from my crown chakra.

Find your mindful moment today

- Book in for some kinesiology, acupuncture or reiki.

- Use a salt lamp to purify your home (salt lamps eliminate toxins in the environment).

- Indulge in a chakra-balancing massage.

- Relax with a crystal light bed therapy treatment.

- Buy some mala beads with a chakra-balancing crystal.

- Block your right nostril and breathe through your left nostril to feel calm.

CHAPTER SIX
BUDDHA BELLIES

i am pure

> *Pregnancy is the time to empower yourself as a woman. You must explore your own limitations and beliefs to develop mental and physical resilience.*
>
> *Yoga gives you the skills to make the birth of your baby and yourself as mother exquisitely beautiful – no matter how it unfolds.*
>
> Nadine Richardson, She Births

Many women start on the yoga path when they become pregnant. A yoga practice connects you to your unborn child and prepares you emotionally and physically for the birth. It teaches mothers how to learn and listen and to rest and nourish their bodies.

Yoga strengthens you and releases tension while uniting your body and mind. You experience a sense of oneness and acceptance.

It can be a very spiritual experience to have another person growing inside you. Another soul is connecting with you. Even if the pregnancy was unplanned, women feel an instant connection.

According to Kundalini yoga, 120 days after conception the soul comes into your baby's body.

Everything you consciously experience while you are pregnant; your state of mind, your relationship to the world and the bond you have with your baby, is all connected. This then becomes the foundation of your child's subconscious, which determines their personality.

Yoga can help you through this life-changing time.

Some women conceive naturally while others go to extraordinary lengths to become pregnant. Either way, your life will never be the same again.

Pregnancy, childbirth and early motherhood are not universally glorious experiences. Recent research tells us that up to 18 per cent of pregnant women are depressed during their pregnancy, and 19 per cent of first-time mothers may have depression in the first three months after they give birth. For 20 to 25 per cent of women, the first three months of motherhood come with mild to moderate levels of emotional distress.

Yoga, meanwhile, can lead you to feel empowered and positive towards pregnancy, birth and being a new mother.

Many women remain disconnected from their pregnancy and even from their child after the birth. Yoga can help us nurture and process what is happening to us emotionally.

We know yoga works by balancing energies in your body and by letting energy flow. This will benefit not just you but also your unborn baby.

You are growing another human being, so during pregnancy you must eat well and rest as much as you can.

If you have an established yoga practice, you can continue this with modifications. But if you are new to yoga, or if the reasons below apply to you, it is recommended to wait until the first trimester is over before starting a practice.

You are advised to <u>not</u> practise yoga in the first trimester if this is your first pregnancy or you have suffered a miscarriage previously or your pregnancy was conceived using IVF.

Pregnancy is a time to slow down. Your body and mind need to be strong. Balance is the key.

During pregnancy, your body expels toxins, making it pure. Hormones are working overtime, which opens up the chakras – the centres of spiritual energy.

Pregnancy is dominated by the sacral chakra which governs your feelings and relationships. This is why pregnancy can be a very emotional time. For some women, it brings great joy; for others, real turmoil.

Some women are so in tune with their feelings during pregnancy, they even know the sex of their child just by using their intuition.

Yoga can be used to balance and refine these energies, emotions and intuitions and much more.

THE BENEFITS OF YOGA WHEN YOU ARE PREGNANT

- It builds up physical strength in your body
- It relieves aches and pains – especially back pain
- It teaches balance – making space for baby
- It can help you open up your hips for the birth
- It relieves stress and anxiety about your pregnancy and the birth
- It helps you to bond with your baby
- It teaches you how to breathe for the birth and pain management
- It teaches you to rest and to sleep when the baby sleeps
- It helps you tap into your intuition – your mother's instinct
- It empowers you – preparing you mentally for the birth

Yoga practice is very much about balance and strength, both physical and emotional and pregnancy is one of the most important times to be balancing and strengthening both of these elements of your self.

❸ Mamata Buddha belly moment

Every night before you go to sleep and every morning before you get out of bed, practise taking three Blissful Belly Breathes (She Births© technique). These are very long, wide and deep breaths into your belly. These are the best breaths for contractions in labour.

Lift your belly as much as you can and slow the breath down as much as possible. Count to 10 with the inhale and the exhale. Visualise a golden light coming into the belly and around your baby; protecting, nurturing and loving them with each breath. Say to yourself that with each contraction, I will breathe long and wide and I will allow my body to do the work. I will relax and I will let go."

....

TIME TO REFLECT

My pregnancy was planned but it took a year for us to conceive. I remember how anxious I felt when it seemed everyone around me was falling pregnant and how trying to conceive consumed my life.

When we are stressed we create an 'unfriendly womb', making it even harder for us to become pregnant. In fact, it was when I finally learned to relax and let go of this anxiety that I actually conceived. And just as yoga helped me make that happen, it also became part of my pregnancy.

I practised yoga every Sunday right up until I gave birth. It helped me to physically make space for my baby and prepare my body for the birth. Emotionally, I felt empowered and liberated to be a woman.

For the first 16 weeks of my pregnancy I felt like I had a terrible hangover – horribly nauseated and utterly exhausted. So I went to Bali on a beautiful retreat in Ubud for a week of yoga, organic food and relaxation and I left leaving wonderful.

During the next few months, I was full of energy and excitement. The last few weeks were heavy and slow, but maternity leave was a beautiful time to reflect and prepare. I birthed my son at 39 weeks.

Expect the unexpected

The birthing experience did not go the way I imagined it would. I wanted a natural birth with lots of being in touch with the process and without drugs. Instead I had a three-day labour with an emergency Caesarean section.

I was exhausted, in intense pain and pumped full of drugs. I was traumatised.

My son was taken away the minute he was born and the whole experience was totally out of my control. The euphoric moment when they hand you your baby for the first time was lost to me. I was affected by the drugs and so exhausted, I could hardly speak.

It took me a long time to get over losing that moment and, in fact, the whole labour and C-section. None of it was part of my birth plan.

All was worth it, however, as Lael arrived a beautiful, healthy child.

My advice is to be open and have no expectations.

Just go with the flow.

Find your mindful moment today

- Lie down and rest.

- Understand that part of the pregnancy process is to feel emotional.

- Find a prenatal yoga class.

- Enjoy a pregnancy massage.

- Create an open birth plan that considers all options.

- Talk or sing to your unborn child.

NEW BABIES, NEW MOTHERS

i am one

You had a Buddha belly and now you have a Buddha baby.

Congratulations.

If this is your first baby, you will have no perception of what it is going to be like. The fact is, there is no manual that covers your experience in particular and every baby is different. Some feed like a dream from Day One, while others struggle for months. Some sleep through the night from early on, while others may take a year or longer to figure out how to do it.

THE SHOCK OF THE NEW

Although it may come easily and effortlessly to some women, most will be shocked by what it means to become a mother.

I am speaking from experience when I say it totally consumes you. The hours in the day – and night – seem to evaporate. Taking a shower and even getting dressed can feel like a luxury, especially when you have been up all night.

If you are a career-orientated woman having a child later in life, the huge change in routine and total lack of control can be extremely challenging – as it can be if you have no family support, a partner working long hours, or no partner present.

For every mother with a new baby, the comfort-zone boundaries are pushed to the extreme.

A NEW SET OF RULES AND TOOLS

These new challenges need a new way of thinking, doing and being.

Once you give birth to your precious baby, you need to look at him or her and yourself and say, "We are all imperfect but we are all worthy of love."

You need to love your child with your whole heart, unconditionally.

You need to believe you are enough – that you are going to be the best mother you can be.

I am also suggesting that even though motherhood is more stressful than you ever could have imagined, yoga will give you the insight and tools to manage this emotional journey.

Try to be mindful not to burden your child with your own stress.

If you are happy and relaxed, your children will reflect this in their behaviour.

Look after you, too

As well as being the most demanding job, caring for your baby is the most rewarding. Yes, you will want to stare at your little package of pure perfection for hours and photograph their every move, but cherishing yourself is also important.

It is easy to put the needs of your baby before your own but if you become exhausted and sick, you will not be able to take good care of them.

In terms of your spiritual energy, it is your root chakra that helps you feel grounded and secure and it is the one that often gets disrupted during childbirth. So, as a new mother, you need to restore your own root chakra energy by getting as much support as you can.

Stay at home as much as possible and get friends to help out. When time allows, cook extra food – or ask someone else to – and freeze it in batches so there are meals at hand on the days when you have no energy left to cook.

Tune in and chill out

Enjoy this time of bonding with your baby. Try not to dilute this connection by being too social or taking your baby to places that will overstimulate them, like shopping centres and other crowded public places. Instead, go for walks with your baby outside in peaceful places. Keep the connection and stay tuned in with each other. It takes time to adjust to this new way of life.

Gently rebuild

After birth, your body needs to be rebuilt. This is so important because many women experience abdominal muscle separation during pregnancy and although the muscles will usually knit back together, for some women the separation is permanent.

There is also the general wear and tear of life with a baby – so many mothers have shoulder and back pain from carrying their little ones – and yoga offers ways for gently rebuilding and strengthening. The poses need to be specific, however. For example, we recommend that you don't do back bends or poses that stretch the abdominal muscles in yoga during this period of recovery after childbirth.

Yoga can also assist emotional rebuilding in this monumentally life-changing situation, while including your baby in the process.

BEING BABY FRIENDLY

Buddha babies thrive best in a calm and loving environment where their connection with their carers and nature is nurtured.

Be sensitive to when your baby has had enough milk, company, excitement or activity. If you become distracted while breastfeeding your baby, for example, that is when they will squirm and become unsettled. Babies do not just need our milk to survive, they need our love, attention and focus in that precious moment.

Avoid overstimulating your baby with constant changes, endless social outings, bright colours and loud noises. This list is a good guide for a calm babyhood.

- ☸ Stick to a daily routine
- ☸ Keep noise to a minimum – speak quietly and softly
- ☸ Do not surround babies with brightly coloured toys
- ☸ Use pastel colours to decorate their room

- Gentle music played softly is like a soothing mantra – its vibration is important
- Stay away from shopping centres and crowded places
- Make a time to connect with your baby without distraction – just the two of you
- Regularly spend time in nature with your baby

Mother and baby yoga

A great way for mothers and their babies to connect is through yoga classes.

I now teach a mother and baby yoga class each week with babies aged between three and nine months old. Once the babies begin to crawl, the class becomes about them, not the mother.

During the class, the babies watch us warm up with a sun salutation dance. As we flow with our breath, we tap the mats and wiggle our fingers to keep the babies engaged.

It calms the babies as they watch Mummy stretch and connect. They observe us as we become trees, poised in contemplation and as we join hands to make a forest. We include the babies as we balance them on our legs while being a graceful warrior and as we work our core using them as weights.

A massage keeps them calm and helps release any trapped wind.

Relaxation ends with our legs resting up a wall with our babies beside us.

It is a beautiful experience for mother and child. I love seeing women, through these classes, release all the stress and anxiety that being a mother can bring.

This class is the highlight of the week for these mothers. We have come to know each other well and regularly catch up over a cup of tea at a local cafe after the class. This sense of community grounds us and fulfils the need to feel supported, just as any mothers' group is a wonderful place to feel connected and balance your root chakra.

☺ Mamata mum-and-baby mindful moment

- Lie on your back with your feet off the floor and your knees bent directly above your hips.

- Place your baby on your shins, holding their arms.

- Move your baby up and down while doing sit-ups to give them a kiss.

- This is a great core workout and your baby will love the motion of being rocked.

MY REFLECTIONS

Following a difficult birth experience I also had real trouble breastfeeding. I expected it would happen naturally but it was actually really hard to master.

My nipples bled for 10 weeks and I would be wincing in pain as I fed Lael every couple of hours. But they eventually healed and I breastfed for nine months. If you are struggling too, then don't be afraid to ask for help. Find your nearest International Board Certified Lactation Consultant – they are the breastfeeding experts.

The breastfeeding problems were just one part of a difficult time and I started to practise yoga a few months after the birth to help my body strengthen and recover and to help me emotionally process what was happening.

I was living far away from my family and my son's father was working long hours so, recovering from a Caesarean section as well, I had almost no support.

On my travels to India and Africa I had seen families and tribes all living together, helping to raise each other's children. Yet in the Western world so many of us seem to be disconnected from our families. If you are feeling lost and without support like I was, my advice is to join a mothers' group. It was my saving grace.

Find your mindful moment today

- Join or create a mothers' group for support.

- Find a mother and baby yoga class to attend.

- Tell yourself every day that you are all your baby will ever need.

- Find some quiet time without distraction to spend with your baby every day.

- Go for a walk with your baby and observe the beauty of nature.

- Sit in a butterfly pose resting your baby's head on your feet and give your baby a massage.

CHAPTER EIGHT

LOVING YOURSELF

i am love

> *Routinely, we spend meaningful time with our loved ones for we know our relationships need this. So why shouldn't we allocate time for the important relationship we have with ourselves? Meditation and mindful living are a chance to make some space for this relationship, which in turn strengthens all our relationships.*
>
> *Sarah Napthali, Buddhism for Mothers*

Yoga teaches that self-confidence comes from within and is not measured by the size of your four-wheel drive, for example. It is a genuine, long-lasting practice of kindness and humility. The best way for you to love your self is to spend time in your own company. For mothers, this is a daily challenge.

YOGI TEA TIME

Take the time, as you sip your tea and relax, to bring your thoughts to yourself – think about loving yourself, like you love your child, that is, unconditionally.

We need to take a pause and have a break.

How can yoga teach us to love our physical self?

- ❸ We learn to love our body
- ❸ We appreciate our body for what it does for us
- ❸ We learn to listen to our body
- ❸ We learn to nourish our body
- ❸ We learn to rest
- ❸ We learn to breathe
- ❸ We learn to listen to our heart
- ❸ We realise we have an emotional, spiritual and physical body
- ❸ We learn how to connect our body, mind and spirit
- ❸ We learn to take care of ourselves

How can yoga teach us to love our emotional self?

- ❸ We learn to observe our thoughts, not indulge in them
- ❸ We learn to choose positive thoughts
- ❸ We learn to just sit and be still in the moment
- ❸ We learn to contemplate and reflect
- ❸ We learn to find balance and focus
- ❸ We learn to be happy for those around us
- ❸ We learn to stop over-analysing and judging everything
- ❸ We learn to cultivate empathy and compassion
- ❸ We learn to feel gratitude and contentment
- ❸ We learn to speak our truth

How can yoga teach us to love our spiritual self?

- We see we are all interconnected
- We see the true nature of reality
- We embrace our greatness
- We let go of attachment and desire
- We challenge ourselves and grow
- We feel unconditional love
- We are mindful and present
- We have no fear of change or death
- We turn intention into action
- We let go of our ego and embrace our true self

JUST 10 MINUTES

It is a challenge for mothers with babies and young children to take time out from their daily routine, but it is vital that you do.

When you take this time – for just 10 minutes – to sit in stillness, you will feel more relaxed and you will cope better with the daily demands of motherhood.

The laundry can wait – washing away the negative self-talk in your mind is far more important.

A mother's love is the heart of the family.

10 good reasons to take a break

- ⊕ You are less likely to shout
- ⊕ You will have more energy
- ⊕ You will feel less stressed
- ⊕ You will feel empathy rather than frustration
- ⊕ You will let go of difficult situations more easily
- ⊕ You will sleep soundly
- ⊕ You will have more compassion towards yourself
- ⊕ You will have more compassion towards your children
- ⊕ You will open your heart and mind
- ⊕ You will experience moments of peace

EVIL INNER SELF-TALK

The way we speak to ourselves has a massive impact on our life because our thoughts become our feelings, which become our words, which become our behaviours. All this will influence the daily choices we make.

As mothers, we seem to be constantly self-analysing, criticising and judging ourselves. We also feel we are being judged and compare ourselves to others. This only increases our negative self-talk, which affects the way we parent our children and our relationships with others.

We have a 'good mother' voice that likes to remind us all the time of our faults, mistakes and bad decisions. "A good mother would not have forgotten his lunch; a good mother would have baked a cake, not bought one. A good mother would not have missed her child's ballet show for an important meeting." We need to ignore that voice.

Look before you leap

You can let go of negative thoughts, and the negative effect they have on your life, but first you need to become aware of what they are. You need to observe them before you live them.

If you wake up grumpy and start acting on that feeling, this will set the tone for the household and it will be reflected in the behaviour of your children.

Instead, take the time to breathe and check in with yourself. Observe the grumpy feeling, think about how your mind works and how you can control your emotions. If you can release the grumpiness now, your day, and everyone else's, will be more wonderful.

Speak your truth

You must learn to speak your truth. This will allow you to live your life from a place of infinite love.

If you are honest with yourself, others will appreciate your integrity and willingness to be vulnerable and you will have great relationships.

An example of speaking your truth is when you order food at a café and it is not to your liking. Do you eat the food, pay for it and leave, unhappy with the experience, or do you explain your feelings to the management?

We are imperfect and that is okay.

If you do not speak up (and most people don't) then, afraid of confrontation and being judged, you are feeding your fears.

If you suppress and do not express your true feelings, this has a knock-on effect and over time, these emotions become toxins that get stuck in your body.

But if you communicate from a place of love and tell the truth kindly, it is greatly appreciated. In the café scenario, a business owner relies on feedback – positive and negative – to help their business succeed and grow.

Adults often do not communicate their true feelings. Kids, on the other hand, tell you exactly how they are feeling. Again, we can learn so much from our children.

THE POWER OF SELF-LOVE

Buddha tells us that if we truly love ourselves, we will never harm another.

When you help yourself you are actually helping others and it will bring you long-lasting happiness.

When you take care of others, you also feel more comfortable about yourself. When you touch other people's hearts, it also heals yours.

Without loving yourself, it is impossible to love others.

☻ Mamata loving kindness meditation

- Place a hand on your heart and close your eyes.

- Repeat the following words silently to yourself as many times as needed.

☻ May I be filled with love.

☻ May I be well.

☻ May I be peaceful and feel at ease.

☻ May I be happy.

The loving kindness meditation above can be practised anytime, anywhere. Once you feel comfortable with doing it, you can start to focus on others – someone who has cared for you, or someone you love. Visualise this person and repeat, "May [his or her name] be filled with loving kindness."

Then, start to visualise someone who challenges you and repeat the above meditation. With practise you can extend this from yourself, to others and to beings everywhere.

The loving kindness meditation helps you feel connected to yourself, others and the world around you.

The power of a loving kindness meditation calms our lives and connects us to our hearts.

There is nothing stronger than the feeling of love.
All our fears and worries disappear in the presence
of love.

TIME TO REFLECT

The best analogy I have heard about being a great parent is during the flight safety demonstrations before take-off on a plane: In an emergency, put your oxygen mask on before putting one onto your child.

You have to look after yourself and love yourself before you can help others. You need to love yourself as much as you love your child.
If you can do that, you are more likely to be a calm parent.

MY REFLECTIONS

When I'm feeling stressed, I'm not a calm parent. And that has repercussions for my son.

If I am calm, he is very affectionate and a dream to parent. But when I am stressed, he lashes out, is more defiant in his reactions and has more temper tantrums. He mirrors my emotions.

I believe a loving mother is someone who takes care of herself so she can take loving care of her children. A mother who takes the time out to soothe her mind, body and spirit will replenish her energy. It will enable her to deal with the challenges the rest of the day brings.

Find your mindful moment today

- Practise the loving kindness meditation.
- Take a break. You absolutely deserve one.
- Put the 'u' back in you.
- Speak your truth and resolve any issues bothering you.
- Love yourself as much as you love your child.
- Remember to always be able to come back to yourself in one breath.

CHAPTER NINE

MUMFULNESS

If a mother values herself,
her children value her.
She teaches self-esteem by her example.
Her peaceful demeanour communicates love
to all who come in contact with her.
Knowing when to sacrifice the self
and when to nurture the self comes from
daily mindfulness.
Vimala McClure, The Tao of Motherhood

Being a mother is like putting your heart in another body and letting it walk around with no protection.

As mothers, the daily emotions we feel are intense and they can swing from bliss to rage in a heartbeat. This is in part thanks to pressure coming from all sides to be a perfect mother while at the same time have a great career, be a loving wife, a goddess in the kitchen and the bedroom and, of course, look like a supermodel.

It's not possible. So you need to focus on your perception of what being a mother is and then let go of what is not working for you.

The thing is, you are already everything you need to be – all the experiences you have had so far have made you the mother you are, and the mother you were meant to be. You don't need to believe it when the media says you need fixing. You just need to reconnect with how powerful you already are.

You have the ability to be a lighthouse for yourself and your family – beaming out a bright light that can uplift everyone around you.

When you rush around engulfed by busy-ness, your light starts to fade. Mundane tasks leave you feeling exhausted and the repetitiveness of the bedtime routine has you gasping for air. Mornings are a military procedure of making lunches while dealing with meltdowns over minor incidents.

Enter the mindful moment.

Mindful moments are all about being absorbed in the present moment on purpose, freeing you from the pain of the past and the worries of the future. This is the true art of paying attention.

You are only truly alive in each moment. In this moment, right now.

Now is when you can appreciate life and what is around you, when you can have meaningful encounters with others.

Now is when you can train yourself to strengthen your mind and create more empathy and compassion within yourself and your relationships. You can let go of judgement and expectations. All you need to do is just notice your thoughts and not be dominated by them.

Mindfulness can be practised by engaging all your senses – taste your food, listen with attention, sense the air you breathe and really see the wonders life offers.

This teaches reflection. If you can learn to quieten your mind and reduce stress, you will be more in control of your own actions. This will make you a great role model for your children.

Be mindful, especially with your children.

You are already enough.

When you are calm, you help create a happier, more balanced child. When stressed, you create stressed behaviour patterns in your children.

This mirroring process shows how connected we are to our children.

So make your day a mindfulness meditation in motion – for your sake and theirs. This can be done while you are cooking, cleaning, chauffeuring, crying or contemplating. Notice how you are feeling. Are you feeling anxious, angry, overwhelmed, elated, frustrated, exhausted or bored? Now, learn to accept these feelings – don't tell yourself what you should or should not be.

You need to reprogram your mind and use triggers so you remember to practise this ancient art and transform everyday life into a mindfulness meditation. Taking a few breaths with awareness each day can help reduce stress and plant the seeds for a practice that nourishes body and mind.

USING YOUR SENSES MINDFULLY

We are bombarded every day via our senses. Studies claim we discard almost 90 per cent of the information overload we receive, which means we absorb only 10 per cent of what we see and hear.

And if we practise using our conscious-awareness mind, we can choose what of this 10 per cent we pay attention to.

Mindful seeing

Eighty per cent of what our brain absorbs is visual and we can find so much joy if we just open our eyes with awareness.

Life moves fast. One day your child is a baby, the next it seems they are off to school. So you need to be very grateful for your eyes. (Not everyone has this sensory pleasure.)

Mindful seeing calms your busy mind by slowing down and simplifying what you see. Go outside and take a breath and absorb the surroundings. There is so much beauty in the world.

Use eye contact with people when interacting with them, especially when talking with your children. Really look them in the eye. Connect and touch their soul. This helps open your heart and instead of feeling anger and frustration, you feel empathy and compassion.

At Rainbow Kids yoga training, the teachers did a meditation where we stood in a circle and spent a minute looking deeply into the eyes of another. It was intense and beautiful. Many of us cried.

Colour, too, has power. You can be mindful when choosing a colour to wear or decorate your surroundings. This can impact you emotionally – different colours can stimulate or sedate, excite or calm, generate feelings of passion or uplift you spiritually. Colour can enhance your social life and improve your state of health. It can be used to develop your self-awareness and make you more feel alive.

Notice beauty.

Mindful listening

You have two ears but when you are having a conversation with a friend or your child, do you really listen? Do you fully engage?

Notice the difference when you are fully present and engaged compared to when you are on autopilot or rushing the kids out the door.

Mindful listening reinforces your emotional intelligence and teaches your children its value.

How many times a day do you tell your children to be quiet? You really need to listen to what your children have to say. The average four-year-old asks 437 questions a day and if you do not listen and answer the little things, they will grow up not telling you the big things. Your children need to feel heard. You also need to be able to sit in silence.

Living with a constant monologue going on in our head, many of us are scared of the sound of silence. But you can learn to sit and just listen and observe the external sounds around you: the birds singing, the wind in the trees, even the buzzing traffic. We can also tune in and listen to internal sounds, like your breath. Your heart beat.

Mindful smelling

A smell can instantly take you back to a distant memory. An aroma can trigger all kinds of emotions. Some scents relax you; others may make you uncomfortable or frightened.

Aromatherapy can play a vital role in your life. Different essential oils can be burned for energy or for relaxation. Scented candles, soaps, creams, perfumes, tea and flowers can all be used in mini mindful meditations.

Pack your handbag with ways to mindfully meditate using your sense of smell. Use a lavender hand cream or honey lip balm and absorb the moment – feel the softness as you rub the cream or ointment into your hands or lips. Really feel and observe the sensations.
Inhale the fragrance and the moment.

Mindful tasting

Too often in our society we overeat and gobble down dinner in front of the TV. We need to slow down, chew our food and taste it, mindfully.

You can learn to savour the taste of food and give your brain a chance to let you know you are full.

Being mindful while you eat and drink with your family also teaches your children to appreciate food and thought. Use the time eating as a family to talk about where the food has come from and about how many people have worked hard to bring this food to you.

Be thankful for food.

Mindful sensation

Our children depend on our love and acceptance, and what better way to show we care than to hug them.

I believe we should hug our children and each other as much as possible. It releases stress and keeps us feeling loved and connected.

Bedtime is great for practising mindfulness through touching. After you have bathed your child, wrapped them in a towel and rubbed them dry, it's time for a cuddle. Pop them into pyjamas, tuck them into bed and read them a story, then it is time to stroke their hair and kiss them goodnight.

Absorb the moment – they are only children for a short while.

Mindful thinking

Be mindful in the way you think.

Are you being critical and judging yourself? Instead, learn to observe your thoughts and choose not to indulge in them.

Sit in silence, rest your mind and start to notice your thought patterns. What are you thinking? Write down your thoughts in a journal and take note of the patterns that arise.

Think about thinking.

Then focus on your breath and start to become aware of your other senses. What can you hear, smell and feel? Do it mindfully.

🫖 Mamata mindful moment

Make a cup of tea.

- Feel your feet and be aware of them stepping on the floor.

- Pick up the kettle and fill it with water. Feel the weight of the kettle in your hand. Place it back down and wait for it to boil, just focusing on your breathing. Watch the steam and wait for the whistle or click.

- Select a beautiful mug and a tea bag. Place the teabag in the mug, pour over the water and watch the tea brew. Add milk if you like, being conscious of the pouring sensation.

- Feel the warmth of the tea as you pick up the mug and take a sip, feeling and smelling the delicate fragrance of the tea. Really taste it.

This may only take a minute or two, but it can be very relaxing. Associate this time with making an intention for the day ahead and visualising what your day will look like.

Create mindfulness triggers throughout your day – the kettle boiling can be one, or set an alarm on a phone or laptop to remind you to be mindful at intervals.

You could even use your mobile phone:
Ring 1 – acknowledge the sound
Ring 2 – notice your breath
Ring 3 – pick up your phone, feeling its weight
Ring 4 – answer being fully present in the moment

And while this trigger could produce an action, it could just be that you simply commit to noticing one beautiful thing.

Children do this naturally – they see the birds in the trees and stop to smell the roses.

....

TIME TO REFLECT

Mindful mothering involves recognising and nurturing your child's full potential. It is not seeing them as a projection of who you want them to be, or of you.

I believe we need to try to be completely present with our children, even if it is for only 15 minutes a day. Give them your undivided attention and listen to their every word. This will help your children feel emotionally secure.

Bake some cookies, read your child a story, build a sandcastle or go for a walk together.

I have learned that when I close my laptop and join Lael in whatever he is doing, being a parent is an absolute joy.

Absorb your children's awesomeness.

....

MY REFLECTIONS

We can learn to mother in the moment by letting go of emotional attachment and labels. By creating a sacred space in your mind, you can then mother from your heart space. When you mother from your heart with unconditional love, your child will absorb this and it will be reflected in heart-melting moments. Notice when they pick you a flower and tell you that they love you or they come into your bed and that adorable little arm reaches out for you.

For me, it is dancing as if no-one is watching in the car with Lael on the way to school.

A mindful mother creates a safe space for her child to be heard and be themselves, so they feel secure and loved.

Lael and I hug every day.

My son is my mindfulness bell.

Ask yourself every day: "What can I do to feel more connected to my child?"

Find your mindful moment today

- Create a mindfulness bell to remind you to be present.

- Use hand cream in your handbag for a mini meditation.

- Give your children a yoga hug and inhale their loveliness.

- Have a mindful cup of tea.

- Put some dark chocolate in your mouth and let it melt slowly.

- For 15 minutes a day be present on purpose with your child.

CHAPTER TEN
CULTIVATING COMPASSION

i am grace

Great thinkers say compassion is the key to a successful society. Business leaders are interested in its potential to reduce exhaustion and poor productivity. Educators know it is what matters most. Scientific institutes are opening new centres to research it. Most of us hold it as a central value in our personal life...

www.compassioninsociety.org

When I went to a Buddhist retreat and learnt the eight steps in training the mind in compassion, taught by Tibetan Lama Sogyal Rinpoche, what resonated with me was how we can apply these teachings to make motherhood less stressful. I have always been drawn to the essence of Buddhism, which is ultimately to transform the mind and find enlightenment through peace, compassion and wisdom.

Awaken your mind and open your heart.

Buddhism teaches us that if we harm others, we are actually harming ourselves and when we help others, this actually helps us.

The first step in practising compassion is to truly love who you are. You can give yourself permission to be happy and take time out for a break. It follows that when you feel good about yourself, you will feel great when you take care of others.

We cannot give to others what we do not already have.

The same applies to your children. If you see your children as extremely kind and full of goodness, that is how they will see themselves and how they will be. On the other hand, if you are always telling your children they are naughty, those words will become their inner voice and they will grow up thinking they are.

You can use positive affirmations with your children every night at bedtime. Get them to repeat, "I am happy, I am kind, I am unique, I am love, I am calm, I am strong, I am wise".

Teach your children to treat other people as they would like to be treated. See them as precious jewels and when they test you, appreciate that they have been sent to teach you how to practise patience, tolerance and compassion. Do not blame them.

See your child as a reflection of you, with the same thoughts and feelings. Just like you, your children simply want to be happy. And don't forget, being a child has its own challenges in this hectic, overstimulating world.

Compassion is also communication. When you speak calmly your children respond much better than when you are shouting. They are sensitive beings, so when you shout instructions to your children from another room it can startle or scare them.

You can show your children real humility by seeing them as superior to you.

You know, your children can teach you so much about life. They see the world through such innocent eyes; observing nature and beauty all around, where we so often ignore it, suffering from our own 'busy-ness'.

To create opportunity for cultivating compassion, replace TV time in the evening with real quality time with your kids. Recent studies suggest the average parent spends less than 49 minutes a day with their child.

For working mothers it is even less. This quality time will often become the best part of your day.

Make the most of your time with your children by being sensitive to what they are feeling. Recognise the triggers for destructive emotions like anger and practise not indulging in these feelings because, like clouds, they are temporary and they will pass. Just like difficult patches in your child's behaviour. Tantrums come and go and children tend to let go of these feelings quickly.

When rushing around dropping off the kids and battling rush hour traffic, let go of stress and worry. Holding onto it harms you and the more stressed you feel, the more your children will absorb this energy, leaving them feeling anxious, too. In turn, an anxious child will project their suffering onto you.

Keep in mind what your child is capable of. They do not develop empathy until they are over four years old as the frontal lobe of their brain, which is responsible for reasoning, is the last part to be formed.

In an argument, teach empathy and compassion by taking the blame even if it was not your fault. Do not be defensive and provoke more anger every time something is broken, a drink is spilled or the couch is jumped on.

Let go of the need to be right all the time. Parent your children like a pilot who is guiding them through life, helping them to become resilient.

By dealing with your own issues through self-awareness you can shift your perspective and change your feelings from being negative to positive.

If you are more conscious of your thoughts you will be more in control of your feelings and reactions.

Remember, your children follow your example, not your advice.

Facing your fears takes courage and strength but with practise you can discover how your own behaviour works and recognise the triggers for anger and frustration. It is so hard to not lose control but yelling at your children does not stop the behaviour that upsets you.

Mamata cultivation compassion moment

After we shout we can:

Calm down together with some mindful breathing

Say sorry that Mum's mind got cross

Make up with a yoga hug

Let go of the guilt, as it only hurts us more.

MANAGING THOUGHTS AND EMOTIONS

It is healthy to express feelings and not suppress them. Conflict is a normal part of family life – there will always be anger – so you need to learn how to manage such emotions.

It all starts with your thoughts. People hold onto their pain and suffering, clinging on to these feelings as if they are a comfort. But what you need to do is practise compassion in such situations:

Let go of blame

Let go of the need to be right

- Let go of criticism
- Stop complaining
- Let go of guilt
- Let go of expectation
- Let go of anger
- Let go of fear
- Let go of excuses
- Let go of ignorance

This list looks all very good on paper but how do we actually manage this in real life on a daily basis?

Learning to let go

The reality is, we are incredibly complex beings and our thoughts and emotions change from moment to moment. We get so lost in our own story. We have no real understanding of who we are. We are born with wisdom but also ignorance. When we are ignorant, we judge.

You can learn to soften and let go of your ego. You can learn how to tame your mind. You can work with anger when it arises and look at the causes and conditions of this destructive emotion.

By seeing what diffuses anger and observing your role in the situation, you can bring in compassion toward yourself and others.

Anxiety and fear come from an irrational or emotional mind. You create so much suffering for yourself when really all you have to fear is your mind.

Living from a place of love

If you transform your mind and practise compassion, you start to live from a place of love.

You can decide if you want to be happy or choose to suffer. Anger is 90 per cent delusion and 10 per cent reality. We worry so much about our lives and we blame others – including our children – for our own misfortunes. We want to block our pain and suffering but by doing that we are blocking our heart and only hurting ourselves more.

You are not your ego

If you lack self-confidence, your ego feeds off that – it becomes your protector.

What appears to comfort you is actually keeping you stuck in the same repetitive thought process.

Your ego is what you project to the world, not who you truly are. You do not need to be dominated by your ego. You can manage it skilfully.

Let go of ego-based self-grasping and self-cherishing. Self-cherishing is not self-love, it is only thinking of yourself.

Self-love is loving yourself so you can love others. If you consider others more important than yourself, then you will cherish others.

Bring on compassion

You can practise compassion on yourself, a friend, your children, an enemy or even people you do not know.

When you watch the news on TV, for example, take on the suffering of others and send them compassion.

We need other beings, including enemies, because without them we cannot practise compassion. They teach us patience and tolerance.

This learning is very helpful when your children are driving you crazy. Be grateful they are choosing you to share their frustration and have kindly given you the opportunity to practise compassion, which opens up the doorway to your heart.

You can practise acts of compassion through everyday events. Use your imagination. Compassion is also communication. True compassion is active.

Practise humility

You can get stuck in your own negative affirmations. Repeating thoughts such as "I am so stressed", "I have no time", "I have no money" or "I am a bad mother" to yourself or out loud to other people turns you into a magnet that attracts suffering.

You need to practise the teachings in this book and feel a difference. You can find liberation through sacrifice. Let go of pride and practise humility. See your own limitations and be respectful of others.

Get some head space

You can get so tired of thinking. This is where meditation helps to regain headspace.

Buddhism sees meditation as a way of returning to our Buddha nature, which is an unaltered, pure state of mind. Our Buddha nature is always there, always pure.

It can be compared to the sky. Some days the sky is full of clouds. We only see the clouds from the ground. Yet when we fly in a plane we discover the sky is infinite and limitless. The clouds are not the sky, they do not belong to it, but they come and go, like our thoughts.

The infinite sky is our Buddha nature of mind. The place in between our thoughts, it is permanent and pure. It connects us with our goodness. It allows us to go beyond ourselves.

Ignorance and delusion prevent connection to our Buddha nature. When our mind settles, we experience contentment and peace. When we discover our true nature, we are blessed with clarity and wisdom.

When your child is having a tantrum, you can practise compassion.

Put your own feelings aside and be grateful that your child feels comfortable enough to express their feelings to you. Expressing gratitude and an appreciation for how your child is feeling takes you out of your own ego and will diffuse your child's anger.

Children feel terrible guilt and shame when they lose control of their feelings, so shouting at them only makes them feel worse.

....

TIME TO REFLECT

I knew a mother who took her son to see a psychologist because he was lashing out at other children and behaving impulsively. One minute he was hugging them and the next he was hitting them. He had learnt that by behaving in a negative way, he got more attention.

Aggression is a normal part of development in some children but there are ways we can help them. We can be more compassionate in the way we react.

The advice from the psychologist was to ignore the behaviour we don't want to see and praise the behaviour we do want to see.

This is compassion in action.

Each morning the first thing I do is switch on my conscious mind. I take a few deep belly breaths and set the intention for the day. I visualise a calm morning that flows before the mind becomes busy with the day's events.

This helps me feel calm, centred and grounded. If I am calm, this will be reflected in my child's behaviour. Each morning I set the intention to be a calm mother.

🧘 Mamata cultivating compassion moment

For a simple exercise in practising loving-kindness, whenever an ambulance or fire engine passes, send out kindness to the people in the vehicle and the people they are going to help. This is great for kids, as they always notice sirens.

My son now always says, "Mummy, we need to say a prayer," whenever he hears a siren.

The power of a loving-kindness meditation calms our lives and connects us to our hearts.

Start your day by setting an intention.

Find your mindful moment today

- Practise a loving-kindness meditation.

- Focus on a friend, child or other loved one to generate compassion.

- Send out loving-kindness with your child when you hear a siren.

- Set an intention each day to be a mindful mother.

- Look at the sky and liken it to your mind.

- Everyone has a story, so be kind, always.

- Get your child to wear a positive affirmation t-shirt as a reminder to be mindful.

CHAPTER ELEVEN

UNPLUG AND PLAY

i am joy

100 years from now it will not matter what kind of car I drove, what kind of house I lived in, how much money I had or what my clothes looked like. But, the world may be a little better because I was important in a child's life.

Author Unknown

According to UNICEF, the unhappiest children in the world are in the UK and the USA – two of the most powerful and among the wealthier countries in the world.

Yet when we travel, we see children in the most impoverished places with smiles from ear to ear. In India, where the majority of people live in poverty, they also live with open hearts and are genuinely happy and kind. Kids play with sticks and stones for hours. Family is strong.

The popular African proverb 'It takes a whole village to raise a child' seems lost in our developed world. Many of us live away from our families and are disconnected from our roots.

This is why we need to support, guide and nurture our children so they feel more able to cope with the inevitable trials and tribulations that life will throw at them.

SAVING OUR CHILDREN

Research suggests that depression is being seen in children as young as three years old. The scariest thing is that children can suffer psychologically without telling anyone or because the issue is not being dealt with.

Children from affluent backgrounds are not immune, often struggling despite being showered with gifts in compensation for the one thing they need most – time with their most important role models; their mother and father.

LEARNING THE LESSONS THAT COUNT

At school, children are taught how to read, write and do arithmetic but they also need to be taught about reflection, relationships and resilience. Compassion and empathy must be taught so they can build and sustain good relationships, whether at home, at school, or out in the world.

ENCOURAGE MINDFUL REFLECTION

Children have the ability to be unstoppable. But because they, as humans, are incredibly complex beings, they need to learn about how their feelings and thoughts work, as well as about numbers and grammar.

As those of us who already have a spiritual practice know, life will always challenge us, no matter how sophisticated or simple, rich or poor we are. So we cannot expect our children to navigate their way through the minefield of life without understanding what being mindful means.

Introduce your child to yoga, which is about being whole.

YOUR JOB AS TEACHER

It's a big job being your child's most important teacher. They need to learn about the workings of their brain, their mind and their relationships; how to discover their specialness, their purpose and their goodness; how their thoughts and feelings become their actions; how to care for their bodies, and develop their intelligence, a social conscience and creativity, plus much more. So let's look closely at your job description as mother.

Teaching about self

Your job as a mother is to help your child discover the best about themselves, so that they understand what their purpose is in life, what their talents are and the best way to use them. You must also help them understand what it means to be a good person, so they need to understand their thoughts and feelings, which will become their actions.

Teaching about body

The problems of unhealthy eating and inactivity are massive lifestyle issues children need to know about. One-quarter of Australian kids are overweight or obese due to unhealthy food choices – being given and choosing highly processed convenience food full of fat and sugar – and a lack of physical activity.

Your responsibility begins with giving your children healthy food from the first mouthful and being a role model in the way you live.

Overweight parents often raise overweight children. And overweight kids become overweight adults.

Be aware of the many health and social problems that come with overweight and obesity, including children being diagnosed with Type-2 diabetes (not the genetic type of diabetes but the type that results from an unhealthy lifestyle).

Show your child what healthy food is and explain that we need to eat a balanced diet to nourish our body and mind.

Teach your child about eating whole foods.

Teaching about physicality, flexibility and resilience

Kids need to be active. They need to be outside playing in nature. Let them climb trees so they learn how to fall and get back up again.

Many children suffer from asthma and allergies. Many are overprotected – wrapped in cotton wool.

Let kids get dirty. This is not only an essential part of play but it will test and strengthen their immune system, too.

The original play station didn't need plugging in – it was known as the backyard, local park, bush reserve or neighbourhood street.

The original play station was playing outside.

Teaching about unplugged fun

Being plugged into technology has had a big impact on all our lives, including the way we read – we now skim and scan information, our minds jumping around like a monkey swinging from one branch to the next.

Screen time is addictive and affects our ability to interact with each other. We just send a text or an email instead of calling or seeing each other. We all desire connectedness but social media disconnects us more than we realise.

Children are plugged in from an early age watching hours of TV, so much of which involves violence, which prepares them for the next transition – video games. Studies show playing violent video games does not necessarily make children violent, but it does show that these children lack empathy. Video games also suppress imagination.

We need to encourage creativity, imagination and the joy of social interaction. Children need to get bored so they can get creative.

Our children are best described as 'tired but wired'.

LESS OVERSTIMULATION AND MORE IMAGINATION

I saw all of these issues in real life when I worked on a summer camp in the USA for children with attention deficit hyperactivity disorder (ADHD). Some of the children needed medication but I am convinced that others were just spirited – like my own son, Lael – and the ADHD label had been applied to take away any blame for bad parenting.

Here in Sydney, children are brought to my classes by nannies who arrive at the family's house at 7am to get the kids up and who are there at night to put the kids to bed because the parents arrive home too late to say goodnight.

So many children are in full-time care from an early age. Once at school, their schedule often includes before- and after-school care, plus an extensive list of extra activities, followed by hours of homework.

At my yoga classes I see the physical effects of all of this and screen-obsession in kids with poor flexibility and a real lack of imagination.

Imagination is everything.

Some parents are too busy even to read stories to their children and many of today's children have trouble sleeping because they are so overstimulated, they just cannot switch off.

Bring back quality time

A friend of mine took her son to a psychologist as he seemed negative and withdrawn. The advice she got was to spend quality time with him, doing whatever the child wanted to do for a certain amount of time every day.

This sounds like a simple thing but in reality it is a significant challenge to consistently find that time. Our children need our love and attention. If we ignore them because we are "too busy", they will feel they cannot tell us the little things that are wrong. Then, over time, they will not tell us the bigger issues they are facing.

Don't miss another heart-melting moment with your children.

Above all, be present

But, you say, I am constantly on the go being a chauffeur, grocery shopping, working, doing housework, being a mother, a wife, a sister, a daughter, a friend... the list goes on. We are bombarded with distractions.

It would be unrealistic in this life for us to be physically present with our children all the time. But when you are with them, be really present.

By being distracted all the time you are telling them they are not important and you are missing precious moments you may never get a chance to experience again. Being present helps us to tune in and feel connected. It also eliminates some of the guilt we feel as parents.

··

TIME TO REFLECT

We seem to have forgotten how to log off, take our child's hand and go for a walk to refresh our minds.

School counsellor and yoga teacher Michelle Ormsby says children don't play in the same way anymore and it's affecting their brains and resilience.

"Creative play is an essential part of child development," she says, "as is learning emotional literacy and social skills.

"In my work as a school counsellor I see children with low emotional intelligence, poor social skills, lack of resilience and anxiety, who feel disconnected. As clinical psychiatrist Daniel Siegel of the Mindsight Institute notes, 'the brain circuitry of resilience can be built through reflective practices and relational skills'.

"In my work, I aim to help children and young people develop and grow through encouraging and nurturing the very practices and skills that Siegel suggests. One of the best tools I can teach children to support this is mindfulness, either of their breath, simply becoming present or through meditation.

"The Smiling Mind program combines mindfulness with technology by offering modern meditations in an accessible and age-appropriate way via an app or the internet, which is how I have been sharing this tool lately.

"My work is like planting seeds with great care in a garden that will grow slowly. Through regular mindfulness and yoga practice, children learn resilience, to calm their minds, feel more connected and to play again, in the present moment."

⊕ Mamata mindful moment in nature

Take your child on a walk and look at all the colours, sights, sounds and textures. Discuss what you can see, hear, smell and feel.

If you prefer to walk alone then go on a silent walk and be fully present. You will be amazed at the beauty you will experience through your senses.

Find your mindful moment today

- Read your child a fairy tale.
- Turn off the TV and get creative.
- Unplug, play and be present with your kids.
- Eat healthy food together as a family.
- Get outside and climb a tree.
- Go for a mindful bush walk.

CHAPTER TWELVE
MINDFUL MONKEYS

> *The future is a mystery, tomorrow is history and today is a gift, that is why they call it the present.*
>
> Author unknown

Babies are born awake, with a Zen-like 'beginner's mind' – they see each moment with fresh eyes, fully open to all possibilities.

Young children are present in the beauty of the moment. Just observe them playing, having a tantrum or laughing uncontrollably. But as they grow up in this society, their minds become muddled with consumerism and conformity. As a result, children develop a 'butterfly mind' that flits from one thing to the next, which makes focusing on one task at a time a struggle.

Teaching children mindfulness allows them to learn how to slow down, focus with purpose and pay attention. In turn, this creates self-awareness.

MINDS MATTER

In her book *10 Mindful Minutes: Giving Our Children – and Ourselves – the Social and Emotional Skills to Reduce Stress and Anxiety for Healthier, Happy Lives*, actress Goldie Hawn says children need to know that their minds matter. She also says they need to be taught how their brain works so they can understand their thoughts and feelings. This is how she explains the brain to a child:

Practising mindfulness is a great way to give your brain a break.

"Your brain is really important, without it you cannot see, hear, run, talk or do anything. It's like a big walnut, but softer, and is protected by your skull. It has two fists called hemispheres.

"Different parts of the brain are responsible for different things. One part, the reptilian, helps you do things without thinking, like breathing and your heart beating. The other side is the emotional brain that tells us how we are feeling. It has an amygdala like a guard dog that barks when something good or bad is happening. Like telling us to smile when we see our friends or run when we are being chased.

"The biggest part is the cortical brain. It remembers things and helps us pay attention. At the front of the cortical brain is the pre-frontal cortex, like a wise owl. It helps us plan, solve problems and make choices. It makes sure our emotions do not take over when we are happy or sad."

To look after that brain on a regular basis, Goldie Hawn recommends we all – children, mothers, everyone – switch off for 10 minutes a day to have a 'brain break'.

MINDFULNESS AND THOUGHTS, CHOICE AND ANXIETY

Mindful awareness is paying attention on purpose to whatever is happening in the here and now, without any judgement. Mindfulness does not aim to change our thoughts – it is about changing our relationship to our thoughts. It shows us that we can choose the path we take and that our thoughts are not permanent.

An important lesson is to understand we do not need to believe everything we think. It feels like our thoughts are very powerful but our thoughts are not facts. We can choose how we respond and react.

We know anxiety is the most common psychological problem in children. That is so partly because our brain tells us what our response should be in certain situations and fear can trigger an irrational emotion. For example, some children have terrible nightmares and get really scared because they believe monsters are living under their beds.

HOW MINDFULNESS CAN HELP

For children with anxiety, mindfulness teaches them not to get caught up in the story – to bring their mind into the present and use it to become aware of the thoughts and triggers that are making them feel anxious.

When the mind is not in the present, anxiety comes from being stuck in the past or worrying about the future.

How do you come back to the present moment? Use your senses and tune into the sounds, smells, sights and sensations that surround you right now.

- If you are depressed, you are living in the past.
- If you are anxious, you are living in the future.
- If you are peaceful, you are living in the present.

Children cannot learn if they are not emotionally secure.

MINDFUL BREATHING

Learning how to breathe mindfully and teaching your child how to do it is a beautiful expression of your love as a mother. It is the ultimate coping mechanism you and your child can use all through life.

Mindful breathing is not just a meditation, it is also contemplation.

As I said previously, mindful awareness is paying attention on purpose to whatever is happening in the here and now, without any judgement. By mindfully breathing for just 10 minutes a day, we strengthen and grow what Goldie Hawn calls the wise owl – the pre-frontal cortex. This allows us to feel positive feelings and dismiss negative feelings. The following mindful breathing exercises are perfect for children.

10 deep breaths to calm down

A simple way to help children feel relaxed and grounded. Speak slowly. Children breathe twice as fast as adults so the trick is to get them to slow down and breathe deeply.

- Breathe in through your nose and out through your mouth.

- This time, breathe in through your nose and as you breathe out through your mouth, make a sighing sound.

- Now, breathe in through your nose and as you breathe out through your mouth, make a sighing sound and focus on breathing all the air out of your tummy.

- Great, that's three times. Let's do seven more...

Breathing games

1. Pretend to blow away the rain – simply cup your hands, breathe in and blow.

2. Blowing bubbles – try to create a really big bubble without it popping.

3. Blowing pom poms and feathers – have a race to see who can blow a pom pom or feather across the room, and then use a straw to make it more difficult.

4. Bubbling milk – use a straw in a tall glass quarter-filled with milk and gently blow lots of bubbles.

Breathing using the senses

Help your kids calm down by breathing through their senses.

SOUND

Bee breathing (Bhramari breath)
This clears the mind and the humming helps children feel relaxed.
Make a humming noise.
Place your hands over your ears and close your eyes.

SIGHT
Breath ball
Use a Hoberman sphere (available from kids' scientific and toy shops) and open and close the ball to represent your belly rising and falling as you breathe.

SMELL
Bunny breath
Take little sniffs of air in through your nose and then breathe out through your mouth.

TOUCH
Hot and cold hand
Put the palm of your hand up next to your mouth and breathe – in feels cold and out feels warm.

Now repeat with your other hand in front of your nose as you breathe in and out.

THOUGHTS
Float away
Think about something – anything.
Now imagine that thought is in a balloon.
Imagine the thought in a particular colour of balloon.

Now imagine letting go of that balloon and watching that thought float far, far away inside it.

Now take another thought and place it on a leaf floating away down a river until it is out of sight.

TASTE
Extreme eating
Sit down at the table with a plateful of small serves of your favourite healthy foods in front of you.

Now take a mouthful, close your eyes and really taste the food as you chew it, thinking about its flavour, its texture, its very own special taste.

Swallow and repeat with each food on the plate, breathing in and out deeply with each thought and taste.

COLOUR BREATHING

This is great for children who are feeling anxious. The colour blue is healing, while breathing out the colour black helps let go of thoughts and feelings.

Close your eyes and as you breathe in, visualise – picture or imagine – you are breathing in the colour blue and as you breathe out, imagine black air is coming out.

Mamata mindful Zen garden making

Making a Zen garden is all about contemplation and expressing thoughts and feelings. It encourages discussion and openness and supports a child in understanding themselves and those around them. It is a wonderful activity that calms and grounds a child. So give your child a few chopsticks, a bowl and a handful of stones or pebbles and let them create a garden design that represents their thoughts and feelings. Any surface will do but you can use sand or gravel or put it in a box. You can add anything that makes your child feel calm.

Talk about their garden with them as they make it, asking them how it makes them feel and what the garden represents. Perhaps it represents friendship, love, harmony, peace. What thoughts are going into your garden? What do those shapes and patterns mean? How does doing this make you feel?

The beauty of a Zen garden is that you can recreate it again and again, using it to contemplate and meditate whenever you need or want to.

This mindfulness technique can also be applied to these activities:

- ☻ Free style drawing using colour
- ☻ Paint some rocks (to put in your Zen garden)
- ☻ Make some friendship bracelets
- ☻ Fold paper to create some origami

MINDFULNESS EXPLAINED IN A STORY

The student asks his teacher why he is always so happy, peaceful and relaxed and the teacher explains how simple it is – that when he walks, he walks, when he eats, he eats, when he sleeps, he sleeps, and so on.

When the student tells the teacher that he does the same, the teacher asks what he is thinking about when he does those things.
The student tells him that when he walks, he thinks about eating. When he is eating, he thinks about sleeping and so on.

Whatever he is doing, the student is not really there – his mind is jumping all over the place, from one thing to another.

A good way to introduce the concept of mindfulness and being present to children is through the book *Mindful Monkey, Happy Panda* by Lauren Alderfer (story) and Kerry Lee MacLean (illustrations). The panda is the teacher and the monkey is the student.

The message of the story is summarised in this quote:

"True happiness comes from bringing all our attention to whatever you are doing right now. There is no need to think about whatever happened yesterday. Yesterday's gone. And there is no need to worry about tomorrow. Tomorrow isn't here. But today is all around us. Bringing your mind back to this moment, right here, over and over again, is called mindfulness."
– Mindful Monkey, Happy Panda

Happiness slips away from us when we dwell on what was, what might have been or what might happen.

☺ Mamata mindful monkey meditation

A beautiful mindfulness meditation to do with children, preferably on a sunny day. Lie on a blanket on the grass next to your child.

Look up at the sky.

See how it changes all of the time.

Some days are grey and cloudy, and we feel heavy.

Other days are bright, and we feel light.

Pretend those clouds up there are your thoughts.

They come and go, they change all the time.

Pick a white, fluffy cloud and breathe into it.

With each breath, see if it changes shape.

Use your mind to focus on it until it floats away.

Now, pick another cloud...

Happiness is right here and now.

☺

TIME TO REFLECT

Everything I recommend here, I have taught and seen how well it works.

One of my favourite classes for children uses the five-senses mindfulness exercise, and it goes something like this...

We close our eyes and listen to the sounds we can hear.

The yoga studio is above a busy road, so we can hear traffic.

But if we really listen, we can hear each other breathing and even our own heartbeat.

We keep listening for the silence between each sound.

We each take a date. We feel its weight, trace our fingers over it, feel the texture, smell its sweetness and study all the grooves of its skin.

We place our date in our mouth but don't start to chew before we have absorbed the taste. Then we slowly start to chew and experience the sweetness.

We talk about where this date came from originally – it started as a fruit on a palm tree in a hot land that had been grown, then dried, put in a package and then sent to a shop. We imagine all the people involved in growing, packaging and bringing us this delicious treat; from the farmer to the person in the supermarket, to the person who bought it for us. We think about their families and the lives they live.

This date represents the whole universe and shows we are all interconnected.

Find your mindful moment today

- Breathe in and out.
- Enjoy a walk.
- Smell some flowers.
- Hug a friend.
- Draw or paint.
- Do yoga.
- Build a sandcastle.
- Watch the clouds.
- Water the plants.
- Make a zen garden.
- Spread some kindness.
- Colour in a mandala.
- Count your blessings.

CHAPTER THIRTEEN

CALM CHILDREN

i am peace

I believe that the purpose of life is to be happy. From the moment of birth, every human being wants happiness and does not want suffering.
The Dalai Lama   www.dalailama.com

Meditation teaches children to find inner stillness and through this, the skills for coping with life. Learning to practise empathy, compassion and the art of reflection helps children to be resilient and form good relationships.

MEDITATION FOR KIDS

Meditation helps bring children into balance emotionally and spiritually. It allows them to let go of overwhelming thoughts and feelings and to manage their emotions. A child who meditates can stay grounded, focused and calm. It helps them learn who they are and builds their confidence. It gives them a sense of purpose and place in this world and a stronger mind to solve the problems and challenges of life.

But meditating with children is not sitting on a cushion in complete silence for half an hour. Instead, children need to be taught how to settle themselves and they need to feel safe as you guide them and show them how to explore their inner self.

You are their greatest teacher, so practise with them until they feel comfortable doing it independently.

TEACHING A CHILD TO MEDITATE

You can teach a child how to meditate and practise mindfulness from an early age because they are already present and their mind is open. Teaching a young child can actually be easier than teaching an adult as they do not over-analyse and judge everything you say.

If you want to meditate with your children, you need to let go of what you believe meditation should be and just observe and accept whatever the outcome is. You may want your child to sit still and be attentive, for example, while they may want to wriggle about and be anything but attentive.

Meditation is a personal choice, however, so suggest some options (see below) and empower your child by asking what they want to do. Keep in mind that if a child is feeling they are being controlled, they are unlikely to settle.

Also keep in mind that, just like you, your child is constantly evolving and will feel different every day. Expect unpredictability and go with the flow – what works one day may not work the next. To begin with, start with a meditation approach that is consistent with your child's age and stage of development

Toddlers

Choose a short and sweet meditation as toddlers may only be able to sit still for a minute. Bedtime is the perfect opportunity to introduce meditation and you can increase the time spent meditating by tiny increments.

Start your story with, "Close your eyes and be very still." Use repetition each time you start and finish by singing or chanting your favourite song. To calm them, rub their third eye centre, which is in between their eyes.

Four to six-year-olds

You can expect a child of this age to sit or lie down for up to 10 minutes, especially during a guided journey or story. See the guided meditation on the next page as a good place to start.

Seven to twelve-year-olds

Do an object meditation and introduce a mantra like "calm" on the inhale and "peace" on the exhale. Counting the breath is also a good distraction for the mind. Start to count each inhale and exhale up to 10 and then start back at one. To challenge your child, start at 50 and count backwards on each inhale and exhale. If the mind wanders, go back to 50.

STRUCTURING THE MEDITATION

When beginning a meditation, it is important for a child to be grounded and centred. The breath is the first stepping-stone on this path for children. It is always with us, anytime, anywhere. The breath also brings us directly into the present moment.

For younger children, get them to place a hand in front of their nose so they can become aware of their breath by feeling it. Make it visual to help them understand the breath. Let them picture themselves blowing bubbles with each out breath. Now, bring focus and concentration into the meditation. Use the other senses and gently guide your child with words and phrases.

To end the meditation, bring your child back gently into the present moment by asking them to open their eyes and to wriggle their fingers and toes.

MAKE A GAME OF IT

Try one or all of these meditation gems with your children. Be sensitive to which one or ones work best for your child. It is okay for this kind of meditation to feel more like calm fun than something really serious. It is a great way to start a lifelong practice that will develop as your kids grow and develop – calmly.

Magic carpet ride

Start by getting comfortable with your child. They can lie down or have their head in your lap. You can make up a story about anything your child loves. Add colour, texture, smells, sounds and a little magic. Here is one to get you started on your journey.

Relax and close your eyes and be very still.

Imagine you are a wizard or a fairy riding on a magical carpet.

The carpet is the colour of the rainbow and feels so soft. As you touch it, you feel calm and peaceful.

This special carpet can take you anywhere you want to go. All you have to do is relax and it will take you flying through the clouds. Hold on tight, here we go.

Can you feel the wind on your face? You are flying through the clouds and you feel so happy. Can you feel the sun on your face? You feel so free.

You can keep flying for as long as you wish and when you are ready you can float back down to your bed.

Now wriggle your fingers and toes, have a stretch and open your eyes.

Lovely listening

Start by sitting quietly with your child.

Close your eyes. What you can hear? It could be traffic, children playing, a clock ticking or birds singing.

Ask them to close their eyes. Ask what they can hear.

Now open and close your eyes again with them. Ask if they can hear the sound of their own breathing. What does it sound like?

Open and close your eyes again with them. Ask if they can hear the sound of their heart beating.

Helping your child gradually bring their awareness within will calm and settle them.

Fabulous feeling

Without your child seeing it, bring a crystal, pebble, feather or other small natural object that would interest them. For this example, we are using a crystal because these little pockets of energy are very comforting for children.

Ask your child to close their eyes and place the object in their hands.

With their eyes still closed, ask them to say or guess what the object is.

Now ask them to open their eyes.

Use the following script, pausing after each sentence:

Imagine you have been given this crystal to look after forever. You need to know everything about it so that even if you dropped it in a pond, you would be able to find it just by looking and feeling.

Notice its shape and colour.

Now, close your eyes again.

Notice how heavy the crystal is.

Feel the crystal all over with your fingertips.

Is it soft or hard?

Is it cool or warm?

Trace your fingers over it.

Is it rough or smooth?

Can you imagine where it came from?

Imagine the sun that has shone on this crystal.

Can you feel the sunshine on the crystal?

How does the sunshine feel?

Imagine all the rain that has fallen on this crystal.

Can you feel the rain on the crystal? How does the rain feel?

Hold the crystal up to your nose. Does it have a smell?

Imagine how safe the crystal feels in your hand.

Hold the crystal so you can feel safe and warm, too.

Keep your child still for another 30 seconds, then gently end the meditation.

Gently open your eyes.

How do you feel inside?

Look at the beautiful crystal.

Does it look any different?

Flickering flame

Sit with your child and light a scented candle.
Both close your eyes.
What does the burning candle smell like?
Now open your eyes and look at the flame until your eyes start to water.
Close your eyes and picture the flame in your mind's eye.
Breathe deeply.
Just sit together and continue to breathe deeply. Your child can watch the flame if they don't want to close their eyes.

Now, do Lovely Listening (see page 152) and at the end, connect with your body.

Before opening your eyes, notice the parts of your body that are connected to the floor.

How does it feel?

If thoughts are coming up, try to let them go and just observe them. Imagine you are blowing them away.

Gently open your eyes.

How do you feel inside?

Shake your mind jar

Make a glitter-and-water-filled mind jar (the recipe is below) and get your child to give it a good shake. The glitter will swirl around the jar – just like the thoughts in a stressed, frightened or too-busy mind – and then it will take about five meditative minutes for the glitter to settle, leaving the water clear.

Teach your child to use the jar to shake away upset, angry or confused thoughts and then become calm as they watch the glitter settle and the water (and their mind) becomes clear.

Children really love this because it is beautiful to watch and it empowers them to have some control over their emotions. And the kids can make their own – just supervise the hot water part and screw the lid on extra tight.

Making a mind jar

You will need:
1 medium glass (or plastic for littlies) jar with tight-fitting lid
1 tablespoon red glitter glue
1 cup hot water
1 tablespoon purple glitter

Add the red glitter glue and hot water to the jar. Stir well. (You will need glitter glue, not just glitter, to help the swirling effect and slow down the settling rate.)

Add the purple glitter, seal the jar tightly, shake and enjoy this sensory experience.

Mandala magic

Colouring in the black and white mandala – or sacred circle – design can be a wonderful meditation practice for children.

Your child can choose a colour based on how they are feeling. As they are colouring, you can ask how it makes them feel.

Once finished, and if it makes them feel happy and safe, your child can gaze at the mandala, using it as an object for meditation.

You can also add the coloured mandala to your child's calm-down corner or box.

Some children may want to use shredding the mandala as a way of letting go of feelings of stress and anxiety.

Mandalas are wonderful for the whole family to enjoy. You do not need a printed design but can make your own by drawing a circle and just letting your intuition guide you. Don't over-think what you are doing, just draw what you are feeling inside the circle. This inspires creativity and can be a healing and calming activity. This is a wonderful opportunity to use the colours of the chakras to teach your child valuable life lessons.

Kids love using colour to learn and they will remember the meanings.

- Red – I feel safe
- Orange – I love my family
- Yellow – I feel strong inside
- Green – I am love
- Blue – I tell the truth
- Purple – I am full of goodness

Let it come, let it go, let it flow.

Learning about rest and relaxation

Children need to be taught how to relax. And once they know how it feels to be calm and rested, they will actually sleep better. In fact, teaching your child to find stillness, as we do in our classes, will reset their body clock for sleep.

Learning to relax and be still will bring benefits to every part of their life and these exercises will make it an easy lesson.

The spaghetti test

Get your child to lie down on their back, then pick up one of their legs and give it a gentle but firm shake. This will release tension and help them to feel relaxed. The aim is to become less like uncooked dried pasta and more like a relaxed and flexible strand of well-cooked spaghetti. Kids love this and find it really amusing.

Do this to each of their limbs until they are relaxed all over.

Rock and jelly

Get your child to focus on a particular part of their body – their arms and shoulders, for example – and squeeze that group of muscles really tight so they feel hard like a rock. Then get them to release those muscles and go floppy like jelly. Get them to repeat the tensing and releasing rock and jelly moves on different parts of their body until they are relaxed all over.

Belly breaths

Pop something light and lovely like a feather, leaf or a small soft toy, on your child's tummy. Now, ask them to breathe in a way that takes the object for a ride up and down on the waves they create with their tummy.

Mamata meditation moment

Children love to draw or write about how meditation makes them feel. They can write their thoughts down in a cloud or bubble. If the drawing represents feelings of sadness or anxiety, your child can shred or tear it up to release these feelings. Discuss these feelings together as a family.

....

TIME TO REFLECT

Our children can teach us so much about life. I believe they choose us. They are only ever lent to us so we should make the most of our time with them.

I have been teaching sisters Lola, 6, and Evie, 4, for over a year. Recently their father told me he walked into their lounge room to find the two girls sitting in lotus pose with their eyes closed in front of the TV.

I hear so many wonderful stories from parents about how their children embrace yoga and meditation.

Enjoy some Mamata yoga stories…

James, 3, now says Namaste when his mummy gives him his dinner.

Jessica, 4, would always say "woof woof" when her mummy wiped her bottom. She couldn't understand why she did this until Jessica told her she was practising her downward dog yoga poses.

A mother was really struggling with her two-year-old, so they developed the practice of holding crystals together to help them calm down in moments of frustration. This worked so well that when her mother started to get frustrated, the child would look at her and say, "stones, Mummy".

I taught a yoga class at a community centre open day. A little girl about seven years old joined in and followed the whole story and was really enjoying herself. After the class, the child's carer told me she was amazed that the little girl had joined in and enjoyed the class so much because she was completely deaf.

I received this letter from one mother who had brought her six-year-old son to one of our classes:

"Since coming to one of your classes my six-year-old son, on his own initiative, has used the calming technique with thoughts floating up in a balloon three different times to calm himself down. He has the mental age of a 10-year-old and his intelligence also means that his ability to generate emotions runs ahead of his ability to calm himself. Because of this, he frequently gets overwhelmed by his emotions, so learning effective calming techniques is really helpful for him."

Find your mindful moment today

- Draw a mandala.

- Make a mind jar.

- Light a candle and watch the flame dancing.

- Play the listening game.

- Do a crystal meditation.

- Write a meditation story for your child.

CHAPTER FOURTEEN
YOUR CHILD
IS YOUR GURU

i am wise

*Yoga lays the foundation
for a lifelong journey of discovery,
familiarity and stability.*
Fenella Lindsell, Founder of YogaBugs

Children are born doing yoga. Babies can go into a meditative state when calm and as they grow, they grab their toes and find liberation performing downward dog.

Children are pure, radiant and full of innate wisdom. Children learn best from their own experiences and from each other by using their imagination. Their curious, intuitive nature makes them the perfect yogi.

Children need to play, exercise, rest, express themselves, shout and release stress. This makes a children's yoga class very different from an adult class. It is high energy, vocal and full of creativity. The use of stories, themes and games captures the children's open minds. But during a class, even though it is active, students have plenty of opportunity to rest and breathe together. In child's pose, for example, they can be a mouse, a rock, an egg or a seed and we use this time to recoup their energy and reconnect.

The beauty of yoga is that it is totally inclusive – any child can take part. It is not dependent on a skill level, physical size or strength; it is not based on good hand-eye coordination; it does not rely on special equipment or large spaces.

As a child grows and develops, yoga continues to offer so much.

Children learn best using their imagination.

Once children start school and the focus moves to literacy and numeracy skills and away from movement and imagination, life for them feels very different – they need an outlet and tools to cope with the inevitable big changes.

The challenges for children are many; from starting a new school, to forming new friendships, to coping with their parents' divorce, to being bullied. They need a way to build confidence and resilience in a non-competitive space.

The yoga community can offer support and a framework for children, no matter what their situation is.

YOGA IS GREAT FOR KIDS BECAUSE...

- They are naturally gifted at yoga
- They are doing yoga before they can even walk
- They are incredibly flexible
- They have little fear, so will attempt any pose
- They have bundles of energy
- They find it easier to meditate, compared to adults
- They have a limitless imagination
- They live in the present
- They are honest
- They have open hearts and minds

Much more than just good fun

Yoga allows children to have fun in a supportive environment while, behind the scenes, all kinds of development is being helped along. Strength, coordination, body awareness, concentration, focus, confidence, social and emotional intelligence and emotional control all flourish. Yoga also benefits creativity, compassion, respect, generosity, self-love and self-acceptance.

Encouraging mental strength and flexibility

By weaving together imagination with relaxation and visualisation, yoga creates a special experience for children.

Through yoga, children are able to learn how to relax. This assists listening skills and makes for better academic and artistic performances. Creating mental images during meditation can help with reading and writing skills.

Yoga teaches children to remain present instead of thinking about what might be happening next. It teaches children about their feelings and emotions so they can have better relationships.

Yoga leaves children feeling happy and content.

Better bodies and health

Children are born to bend and stretch but as they are spending more and more time sitting at desks at school and in front of computers, their posture is starting to change. Even by the age of five, some children cannot touch their toes.

Yoga counteracts this trend and improves flexibility.

Children naturally love to play different sports and yoga assists with agility and injury prevention in sport.

Yoga supports a healthy immune system and good sleep patterns by toning the parasympathetic nervous system. High-energy classes that end with a relaxation session leave children feeling relaxed and calm.

Better behaviour

It's fascinating to watch children with shyness, anxiety or a behavioural issue of some kind change week after week with each yoga class.

A shy or nervous child may sit back and watch for a few weeks, then become the one at the front, leading the class. Disruptive children like to be challenged with poses and praised for executing them. An energetic child will often be the one who falls asleep in relaxation.

Yoga can exhaust normally over-exuberant children who, after leaping around and stretching themselves, just want to rest and have time out from their overscheduled lives.

So much to learn

In yoga, children fly on space ships or magic carpets, discovering different cultures and learning about the world we live in. They learn about nature and how to care for their planet. They love the many facts and figures about animals we share with them and the way their body works will always fascinate and engage a child.

Yoga engages all the body systems – the skeletal, circulatory, nervous, digestive, respiratory, hormonal and muscular – and teaches children about their own anatomy.

Yoga is non-competitive and any child can do it.

Importantly, children also learn that even though we all look different, inside we are all the same. We all feel love and pain and we are all connected.

Caring and cooperation

Classes include partner work which encourages trust and respect for each other and promotes teamwork.

YOGA IS FOR ALL KIDS

In teaching kids' yoga classes in childcare centres, preschools, primary schools, after school and school holiday programs, community centres, at events and festivals and even at birthday parties, we have all kinds of kids and ages covered.

Toddler yoga

Yoga helps toddlers land in the body they were born into.
It helps them become aware that their arms and legs are connected to their body.

Yoga imprints on their minds, helping them with their balance and physical coordination, keeping them grounded.

The faster toddlers connect with their body, the better they feel within it. And once a two-year-old discovers they can actually do yoga, it will be something they will do every day, without instruction.

Yoga empowers children because it is something they can do with ease.

The stories and songs we use in children's yoga encourage language and social development. This stimulates emotional and linguistic development which promotes confidence and self-esteem.
The movement of yoga strengthens muscles, balance and coordination in toddlers.

Carers join in and children learn through repetition and imitation, not through explanation.

Classes are structured to include a warm up, story adventure and a relaxation period which often includes a massage between mother and child.

Children are taught about the breath and how the way we breathe affects the way we feel. To encourage this learning, we make it visual and interactive with props like feathers, leaves and straws. Puppets, masks, books, stickers and yoga cards are used in the process.

Preschooler yoga

Classes for this group are high energy as these children have infinite amounts of energy and incredible imaginations.

Preschoolers like to stretch up to the sky, tap their bodies, shine like stars and blow away the rain. Singing songs and counting will engage them and keep them in a pose for longer.

It's so much good fun stomping around the room like bears or pushing against a wall to open the door to a giant's house.

Yoga at this age needs to capture a child's innate curiosity and foster their imagination. It also teaches them to follow instructions – if you tell a child they are hiding from a dinosaur, they will hold that pose until they are instructed to come out of it.

At this age, props are used to demonstrate the breath and how the body works and children can relax with mindful activities like making a Zen garden or drawing a mandala.

Games are played that stimulate trust, intuition and gratitude. Classes end with a guided visualisation or meditation using music or an object. Placing a magic stone on a child's forehead will keep them still and massaging their feet and stomach or back helps them to relax.

Yoga for five to eight-year-olds

Active imaginations are fuelled by classes themed around journeys. Partner work is introduced and used to entertain and engage. Games are played to test memory, create poses, mirror each other and work together as a group.

Children play follow the leader, taking it in turns to lead, promoting confidence and trust. Whispering, dancing, clapping and body drumming all engage the children.

We teach the children to sit quietly and focus inward and enjoy a longer relaxation using an eye pillow. A peace mat is used for children to take a break or calm down if they need to.

Yoga for eight to twelve-year-olds

We use a unique combination of posture and partner work to challenge children of this age group. Classes are structured around concepts and sequences that include problem-solving tasks, designed to develop trust and connection while supporting each other.

Mindful meditations using crystals and pebbles help ground and focus children, especially after a long day at school. Classes include games, creative movement, massage, acrobatics and building a human pyramid.

This age group wants to feel in control, be physically challenged and mentally stimulated. They like classes that are fun and cool.

Teen yoga

Kids at this age want to be respected and treated like adults. So classes can start with a meditation or centering activity and are much more like an adult yoga class but still include partner work, cooperative games and a focus on quiet time.

GAMES TO ENGAGE AND CHALLENGE CHILDREN

Try these games we use in classes to challenge and occupy your child at home.

Toe-ga

Pick up cottonwool balls using your toes. Using the toes stimulates the brain and the deep breathing that comes with the effort and concentration switches on the parasympathetic nervous system, which has a relaxing effect. This game is excellent for concentration.

Ring-for-a-hug bell

Use a bell that your kids can ring whenever they want a hug from you. If you are feeling stressed then ring the bell and child will soothe you with a heart-melting cuddle.

Farmer and a seed (for pairs)

One child is a farmer and the other is a seed. The farmer helps the seed grow into a tree. The seed receives sun (arms reach up high), rain (tap fingers on seed) and love (hug seed).

At the end of this game, as a reward, we give the children foot massages and rub their ears to help them relax.

Human mandala (for groups)

We were inspired by the Rainbow Kids yoga program to do this activity. A mandala is a meditative circle-like pattern.

Sit together with legs crossed and knees touching, so everyone is connected. Start to stretch together in unison. Create a beautiful seated dance and do yoga moves, playing follow the leader like a Mexican wave.

Crab soccer

A fun and high-energy game where two teams get down into 'crab' or table-top position, sitting on their bottoms on the floor with hands positioned behind and moving around using only their feet to kick a large, soft ball.

Yogi says

Based on the game Simon Says, this is played doing yoga poses. It allows children to show off and recall their favourite poses.

USING PROPS

We like to use objects to help demonstrate how the body works and to make the act of breathing more visual for children. This is so they can understand how the way we breathe changes the way we feel.

Mind jar

This glitter-and-water filled jar helps everyone feel calm. See page 155, in the Calm Children chapter for instructions on how to make one.

Pass the chimes

Another good game for keeping children focused and calm is to pass and ring a set of chimes.

Use two small chimes attached with leather. Ask your child to hold the leather and gently ring the chimes and pass them on. It takes concentration to get the chimes to meet at the same time. It makes a beautiful sound. A harder version is to pass the chimes without them touching.

Yoga cards

Using animal cards, children pick a card with an animal on it and do the associated pose. Exploration cards are used to discuss the meaning of love, gratitude, wisdom, adventure, stillness and acceptance.

We use these with children to create a story and also to play memory games.

Yoga dots

Yoga dots are small circles made from a yoga mat that give younger children a focus point and a place to return to.

Place the dots in a circle and get the children to jump around them like frogs on lily pads. The children can also roll them up and use them like a telescope, or use them like a pillow to rest on. School-aged children prefer to use an adult yoga mat.

Yoga sushi

Roll children up in a yoga mat to make yoga sushi. This sensory exercise is really fun and helps children feel safe and grounded.

YOGA FOR GIFTED CHILDREN

We want to empower children and teach them they are special and unique, no matter what they look like or where they have come from.

Breathing techniques help children on the autism spectrum and with ADHD to focus and feel calm.

POSITIVE AFFIRMATIONS

We use positive affirmations because what we think, we become.

Children can be taught that they have control over their thoughts, which affects how they feel. They can choose to be positive and this can bring out emotional, physical and mental changes in them.

Positive affirmations help us to feel better and happier about ourselves. This will help children grow into successful, fulfilled adults.

Here are some simple positive affirmations to do at home:

- ☻ I am kind
- ☻ I am happy
- ☻ I am strong
- ☻ I am peaceful
- ☻ I am relaxed
- ☻ I am a good person
- ☻ I am kind
- ☻ I am smiling inside
- ☻ I am lovable
- ☻ I am enough

☻ Mamata mindful moment

Put some simple affirmations on the wall in your child's room as a reminder for them to be a good person. Give them gentle guidelines and rules to follow.

For younger children, get them to straddle your lap and then, while they are there, roll up and down on your spine on the floor or bed, repeating the affirmations. Your child will love the connection of being close to you, the rocking will massage your back and it is a good core workout for you.

Here are some simple affirmations to start with:

- ❂ Be happy
- ❂ Always tell the truth
- ❂ Keep your promises
- ❂ Help others
- ❂ Say please and thank you
- ❂ Laugh a lot
- ❂ Try new things
- ❂ Spread kindness
- ❂ Count your blessings
- ❂ Smile

FAMILY YOGA

Family yoga is a wonderful activity for the whole family, including parents, siblings, aunties, uncles, cousins and even grandparents.

It strengthens family bonds, is fun and healthy and promotes connection, compassion and community.

The classes are structured in the same way as a children's class, because so much of what we teach and share with children also has huge benefits for adults.

As adults, we seem to have forgotten how to play and have fun and this class helps us find our inner child.

It also allows us to teach parents that their child is their guru. When parents become children and children play the leader, the role reversal breaks down barriers and empowers kids, while parents understand what it is like to be a kid again.

LEARNING TOGETHER

Partner poses, deep breathing together, games, dancing, laughing and having fun all create a unique and dynamic environment for everyone to learn and share together. Parents are taught breathing exercises and mindfulness practices that they can do at home together as a family.

During relaxation, children can lie down next to their parents or help by placing eye pillows on them or massaging their feet. They get to wake up their parents with cuddles and kisses.

Family yoga is also a great time for like-minded families to connect and share their journey of parenting. Friendships are formed and a community is created.

FAMILY YOGA AT HOME

Keep feeling the family love with these mindful at-home practices.

Mindful mealtimes

Meal times are a great time to practise mindfulness and connect as a family. Discuss where the food you are eating has come from and express your thanks for the food.
Use this time to discuss how everyone is feeling and go around the table and get everyone to say what they are grateful for.

Calm corner

Create a calm-down corner in your home using a bean bag or yoga mat and a small table. Children can have a calm-down box for special objects like a crystal or cuddle toy and they can decorate this special place with flowers, candles, drawings, pebbles or anything that makes them feel relaxed.

Yoga and meditations

Flip through this book and do any of the meditations or mindfulness practices you like together as a family.

Yoga is always better when shared, so roll out your mat and encourage your child to join in with you.

⊙ Mamata family yoga moment

Lie down on your back. Get your child to lie down next to you and put their head on your stomach, so they can feel your belly moving up and down as you breathe.

The weight of your child's head will help you breathe into your belly and your child will be calmed with the rise and fall of your breath. Get the whole family to join and make a human staircase.

TIME TO REFLECT

Teaching children yoga is an uplifting experience that nourishes my soul because their energy is infectious. Children teach us so much about life because they see it from a beginner's mind. When I am reading Lael a story and I forget a word or miss a page, he always corrects me because he lives in the present moment. He also always remembers where I have parked my car, which is very helpful.

Of course, sometimes children do not listen and are disruptive and the class plan is that there is no class plan. This is so especially if it has been raining for days and the children have not been outside, or when there is a full moon. At times like this their energy can be frantic but it has taught me to go with the flow and be spontaneous and creative.

If the children need to run around and let out their pent-up energy, then the class will reflect this. If they are tired but wired, we play a high-energy game, like musical yoga statues and then have a longer relaxation.

Children lead the class with their intuitive and curious nature. Children also share their feelings in this environment. I am their yoga teacher, not their school teacher or parent. They are able to be open and discuss how they are feeling, which creates a beautiful relationship between teacher and student.

Teaching children yoga healed my heart.

Find your mindful moment today

- Write some positive affirmations.

- Make up a story using some yoga poses you know.

- Play the farmer and seed game.

- Make some yoga cards.

- Do some fun family yoga.

- Using your fingertips, gently 'write' I love you on your child's back.

CHAPTER FIFTEEN
BE THE LIGHTHOUSE

i am light

Being a mother is such an important role and comes without any training. A mother's love is the heart of the family.

But the role of mother is a challenging one. We are not always perfect and spend many hours a day worrying about our choices and decisions. We put everyone else's needs above our own and work tirelessly to fulfil those of our children.

Motherhood is a life sentence – once a mother, you are a mother for your whole life. It is a mixture of laughter, promise, stress and tears. Your greatest joy but also your deepest sadness.

CONNECTING WITHIN AND WITHOUT

Although the mother-child relationship is a profoundly important one, mothers and children need to find love within themselves as individuals and in other relationships in the outside world.

As mothers, we need to break down the barriers we create around our children and ourselves.

The entire purpose of doing any kind of spiritual practice is to feel more connection within ourselves and with the world around us. By discovering a higher purpose, we become conscious and understand that we are so much more than just our physical body; that we are all connected through spirit. All we want is to feel a sense of purpose and belonging.

The ancient practices of yoga, meditation and mindfulness can provide a way for us to heal ourselves and make sound connections – among them, those that show us that every mother experiences the same frustrations and the same triumphs and that single or married, we can still feel alone.

A spiritual path teaches us that we do not need to rely on others to feel love. We can create this within ourselves and this will strengthen our relationships with our loved ones.

EMPATHY, NOT OWNERSHIP

When we see imperfections in ourselves and in our children, we need to be mindful.

Mindful parenting advises us to see our children as their own entity. We do not own our children, we cannot stop them making mistakes as they learn what they need to know in life. We must let them live their lives.

Instead, we need to cultivate empathy. Ancient wisdom tells us to understand that we will make mistakes and our children will make mistakes and we need to practise acceptance and not judge them or ourselves. Life is the way it is and our children are not a judgment of who we are, or us of who they are.

FLY ABOVE THE CLOUDS

Life can be a daily struggle. We get situations thrown at us from every angle and we need coping strategies. In hard times, we can teach ourselves to rise above our situation, just as pilots are taught to fly above the clouds, not straight through them and certainly not underneath them.

When things get tough, we need to elevate ourselves and fly higher. We can do this by opening our hearts and minds. These spiritual practices plant the seeds that can allow us to cleanse our life and free ourselves from the suffering we create. The suffering all starts with our thoughts.

THE THING ABOUT THOUGHTS...

- ☸ Our thoughts are not facts but we believe them and they rob us of our freedom.

- ☸ Our thoughts are sparks of energy that shape our reality, so we have the power to create a successful and happy life.

- ☸ Our minds are made up of our thoughts, beliefs and self-talk. What we think, we become.

- ☸ Our thoughts manifest into the universe and have the power to bring material things into creation.

- ☸ The types of thoughts we have determine the type of person we are and the reactions we have to the outside world.

- ☸ The types of thoughts we have reflect how we live and the people with whom we associate, and will influence our decisions and actions.

- Positive thoughts give us energy and we feel light and free. If we wake up in a good mood, feeling energetic, our daily routine will flow well and this is reflected in how we feel. When we get out of bed on the wrong side, the day can unfold with constant drama and challenges.

- The way we feel and act has a knock-on effect with those around us, especially our children.

SOBERING STATS

According to cognitive scientists, we have about 60,000 to 70,000 thoughts a day – that's one thought per second during every waking hour. Within those 60,000 thoughts, 95 per cent are the same thoughts we had yesterday, and the day before, and the day before that.

Our mind is like a record player, playing the same record over and over again. This would be a wonderful gift if we had trained our mind to be present and think positive thoughts, but our mind wanders at least 30 per cent of the time and 80 per cent of our thoughts are negative ones.

STOP THE THOUGHT WARS

We fight a constant battle with others and ourselves in our mind by judging and over-analysing everything. We hold on to anger and frustration, which hurts us, and then we project this suffering onto others.

We do not need to believe everything we think. Constant negative thoughts create patterns and habits that, over time, create unconscious and automatic negative emotions. These emotions become toxic and get stuck in our physical bodies, which manifests into disease – it could be a nasty cold or it could be much worse, like cancer. To stop this war, we need to start with ourselves. This is what a spiritual path allows us to do.

ON THE TIP OF AN ICEBERG

We have created unconscious unhealthy habits that we do not even think about while we are doing them. This could be the way we breathe, our posture or the way we get annoyed and shout at our children.

The first step towards breaking these habits is to become conscious of them. Our conscious mind is the tip of a huge iceberg – our unconscious thoughts being the huge mass below the surface.

Yoga poses are also the tip of an iceberg where the philosophy underlying them can do an immense amount for us on the emotional and spiritual level.

Practising yoga and meditation is not about trying to resist our bad habits; it is about consciously practising good habits that re-wire our brain, so good habits happen unconsciously.

LEAVING THE LOOP

Our thoughts create our emotions, our emotions create our thoughts, and we get stuck in a loop that takes us nowhere. But we can change our thoughts, which will change our feelings, which will change our behaviours.

Being mindful is the key. When we are mindful, we can think about our response – is it going to serve me well to react like this?

Remember always that words are a projection of our thoughts and they have tremendous power. So if we can change the way we speak and react to others and ourselves, we can change the way we feel and live.

CREATE A POSITIVE STORY

Our throat is the doorway to our heart. If we keep saying we do not have enough time or money, then we will manifest this into the universe and this is how our life will play out.

If a woman tells herself she is not a good mother, she will believe those words, feel like a failure and be consumed with guilt.

We need to stop putting a Band-aid on our problems and go to the root of them. We need to look at the story of our lives so far and reflect on what our thoughts and feelings are creating for us. What we do automatically, without even thinking about it, will tell us the habits we have created for ourselves. Keep a journal to see how the story of your life is playing out.

ATTRACT ENERGY YOU LIKE

The law of attraction is the name given to the belief that 'like attracts like', and that by focusing on positive or negative thoughts, one can bring about positive or negative results. This belief is based upon the idea that people and their thoughts are both made from pure energy, and the belief that like energy attracts like energy.
Our life will change if we shift our perceptions.

Our purpose in life is to open our hearts.

BE MINDFUL AND LET IT FLOW

Feeling content with motherhood plays a huge role in our happiness levels. Learning to let go of what is not working for us anymore and focusing on what is helping us to grow is a profound lesson.

Life changes; it is always unpredictable and full of surprises. But if we adopt the mantra 'Let it come, let it go, let it flow', when challenging situations arise, we do not need to get caught up in our emotions. We can respond and not react by being mindful in that moment. We can pay attention to what is happening and how we are feeling without making any judgement. We can teach ourselves to respond and to not react.

FIND MEANING IN THE PAUSE

We are told so often to 'keep calm and carry on'; to soldier on regardless of what is going on around us. But this approach will surely lead us to a mental or physical breakdown.

We need to take a pause and check in with what we are feeling.

Soldiering on year after year renders us totally depleted even before the baby arrives and so many women never catch up before they have another.

So often our lifestyle robs us off the energy to cope with the stresses of it. We drink too much, eat processed foods, do not sleep well and slave away in our jobs, which are often meaningless.

Stress manifests in our bodies and makes us sick. When we are sick and have no energy, we struggle to remain calm. We need to find moments in our day to feel calm, because motherhood requires an abundance of perpetual energy.

TURNING ADVERSITY INTO OPPORTUNITY

The most difficult times in life are the best chances to gain real experience and great inner strength. These times can actually help us profoundly. Important spiritual lessons are being learnt.

Challenging times provide us with the opportunity to understand what it means to suffer and to inspire compassion. Even though we go through a necessary process of denial, anger and acceptance, we can come out the other side filled with gratitude. These challenges can open our hearts.

Embrace your vulnerability

Having a child makes us vulnerable by pushing us to our limits. Boundaries are tested, along with our relationships and we try to suppress these feelings.

But, being vulnerable makes us 'whole-hearted'. Being whole-hearted, a word used by social researcher Brené Brown, gives us a sense of worthiness, courage, compassion and connection.

It takes courage to be imperfect and compassion to be kind to ourselves and others. Being vulnerable can be the birthplace of something beautiful. It could lead us to having a spiritual awakening. And so can becoming a mother.

LIVING WHOLE-HEARTEDLY

After reading this book, you will know how to find many calm moments of reflection in the day, but all it takes is just one moment a day to connect with ourselves and our children. Mothers don't have much spare time, but you can always return to yourself in just one breath, in a single moment.

Create some principles to remind you how to live from a place of love in a whole-hearted way – how to live with an open heart and conscious mind.

🧘 Mamata mindful message

Return to this page often to be reminded of what matters in a mindfully-lived, whole-hearted life. These principles apply in every moment, every day.

- 🧘 Be present – presence has power and all we ever have is the present moment. Be present, especially with your children.
- 🧘 Spread kindness – it has been scientifically proven that performing random acts of kindness releases serotonin, which is a hormone that relaxes us. Teach your children kindness, too.
- 🧘 Respect yourself – and be compassionate towards yourself.
- 🧘 Speak your truth – express yourself with honesty and grace.
- 🧘 Live with intention – an intention every day that works for you: to be a loving mother, to do your best, to take a break, to love yourself, to be mindful, to be calm, to be compassionate, to breathe deeply...

- Be grateful – gratitude is magic because it turns what we already have into enough. Say what you are grateful for every day around the dinner table.

- Meditate – calm your busy mind with mindful meditation you can do anywhere, any time, even with your child.

- Breathe deeply – on the spot, with intention, or make the time to go to a yoga class. Breathing deeply in yoga will balance your energies and keep your body, mind and spirit connected. Do yoga together with your child or as a family.

- Practise acceptance – truly love who you are and then you can extend this love to others. Accept your situation for what it is and your children for who they are.

- Be positive – be mindful of your thoughts and words, as they create your reality. Use positive affirmations for yourself and with your child.

- Find your light – be the lighthouse and shine brightly, uplifting yourself and all those around you.

WHERE TO FROM HERE?

Thank you so much for taking the time to read *Mother Om*. I truly hope you have been inspired and encouraged to take the first steps along a spiritual path, keeping in mind that each person's journey and experience is unique, and that you need to choose your own path.

This book has described how yoga, meditation and mindfulness can offer a harmonious and healthy lifestyle for you, your child and your whole family. These practices will increase your capacity to love yourself so you can then extend this love to others. Of course, being 'practices', they need to be done regularly for you to reap the benefits.

Committing to a daily practice with intention is the key to activating the life changes you desire. You are in control of your thoughts and feelings and together we can create a society that thrives upon compassion and connection.

I look forward to welcoming you to our community of like-minded families who celebrate the goodness of life and cherish our children together.

⊛ Mamata mala moment

Purchase some mala beads from a spiritual store. Take a string of mala beads, which contain the auspicious number 108. Place the beads over the ring finger of your right hand and sit quietly. Use your thumb as you turn each bead, using the mantra 'Ma Om' – 'Ma' for one bead and 'Om' for the next.

This mantra comes from the secret language of the heart and it encourages us to be peaceful mothers. This was given to me by one of my teachers who was given this by Mother Maya, a renowned spiritual teacher. So, now I pass this on to you, with love.

Keep your beads close by and use this mantra whenever you feel the need to find mindful balance.

MY FINAL REFLECTION

In moments of intense darkness we can see elements of our soul that lead us to discover our truth.

So many of us live in our darkness and we use our fear like a heavy curtain. We shut out our light.

In a room full of darkness we can always see the light, shining through the cracks.

If we embrace our light, our light grows and the darkness fades. We all have a light inside us.

I am not afraid of my darkness any more. In fact, there have been times when I have been more afraid of my light. It shines like a diamond and it is overwhelmingly beautiful.

Our darkness makes us appreciate our light, and our light gives us gratitude for our darkness. It shows us our true potential is limitless.

Mothers have the power to be a lighthouse – to lead, uplift and heal others with their compassion and grace.

A mother's love for her child is her yoga practice.

As a mother, you are the whisper in your child's ear, the soft breeze in the trees, the smell of a dozen roses, the fragrance of love. You are a gentle hand on a runny nose and a knitted scarf on a winter's day. You are the sound of rain running down a window and the joy of seeing a face in a fluffy cloud. You are the pot of gold at the end of the rainbow. Your touch calms and soothes and you make the world go around. You are your child's first love, best friend, first enemy, first guru. You are irreplaceable.

You are Mother Om.

Om.
The universal sound of creation and peace.

Namaste

REFERENCES

The ideas in this book come from my many hours of studying yoga and meditation and from my own personal practice. Below is a list of books and websites that I highly recommend for further reading and services that can help guide you along your path of being a peaceful mother and raising content children. These are correct at the time of printing. There is an abundance of knowledge online so find the connection that is right for you and enjoy.

1 – MAMATA YOGA
Teacher Training
Sukha Mukha teacher training manual   www.sukhamukhayoga.com
Yoga, Tantra and Psychology course - Natalia Perera   www.saffronrose.com

Reading
- Manitsas, Katie, (2010) *Yoga off the Mat – Inspiration and support for living your yoga every day.* LYL PUBLICATIONS.
- Iyengar, B.K.S (2002) *The Tree of Yoga.* SHAMBHALA PUBLICATIONS.

2 - PRINCIPLES OF YOGA
Reading
- Satchidananda, Sri Swami, translation and commentary - (2011)
  The Yoga Sutras of Patanjali. PUBLISHED BY INTEGRAL YOGA PUBLICATIONS.
- Lindsell, Fenella. (2008) *YogaBugs – The one bug your kid should catch.*
  VIRGIN BOOKS.   www.yogabugs.com.au

3 – YOU NEED TO RELAX
Reading
- Siegel , Daniel J (2012) - "*The Developing Mind*" 2nd Edition
  THE GUILFORD PRESS   www.drdansiegel.com

Programs
Katsikis, Sandra , (2013) Stretch and Connect program
www.soothingsouls.com.au

4 – MAMATA MINDFUL MEDITATION

Training

Mindfulness Training by Paul Von Bergan

Billabong retreat   www.billabongretreat.com.au

21 day meditation challenge Oprah Winfrey and Deepak Chopra

www.chopracentermeditation.com

Mindful in May   www.mindfulinmay.org

Head Space   www.getsomeheadspace.com

Reading

- Willard, Christopher.(2011) "*Child's Mind – Mindfulness Practices to help our children be more focused calm and relaxed.*" Parallax Press.

www.drchristopherwillard.com

5 – SPINNING WHEELS OF ENERGY

Courses

Natalia Perera   www.saffronrose.com

Daphne Ravey   www.shaktibliss.com.au

Patty Kikos   www.pattykikos.com

Reading

- Anna Selby, (2009) *Total Chakra Energy Plan – The practical 7 step program to balance and revitalise.* Duncan Baird Publishing.

6 – BUDDHA BELLIES

Reference

Nadine Richardson   www.shebirths.com.au

Reading

- Manitsas, Katie, (2010) *The Yoga of birth – sacred wisdom for conception, birthing and beyond.*

7 – NEW BABIES, NEW MOTHERS

Reference

Daphne Ravey   www.shaktibliss.com.au

Brené Brown   www.brenebrown.com

8 – LOVING YOURSELF

Reading
- Sarah Napthali, (2003) *Buddhism for Mothers – A calm approach to caring for yourself and your children.* ALLEN AND UNWIN.
- Kornfield , Jack (2002) *A Path with heart – The classic guide through the perils and promises of spiritual life.* RIDER BOOKS.
- Rinpoche , Sogyal, (2002) *The Tibetan book of living and dying. 20th anniversary edition.* HARPER COLLINS. www.sogyalrinpoche.org

9 – MUMFULNESS

www.mindfulmomsnetwork.com

Reading
- McClure, Vimala. *The Tao of Motherhood. 20th anniversary edition.*
- Dwyer, Kim and Reynolds, Susan. (2012) *Meditations for Moms – How to relax your body, refresh your spirit mind, and revitalise your spirit.* ADAMS MEDIA.

10 – CULTIVATING COMPASSION

www.compassioninsociety.org

Courses
7 steps to training the mind in compassion retreat
Sogyal Rinpoche   www.rigpa.org

11 – UNPLUG AND PLAY

Smiling Mind   www.smilingmind.com.au
www.mindsightinstitute.com   Dr. Daniel Siegel

12 – MINDFUL MONKEYS

Reading
- Hawn, Goldie with Holden, Wendy (2011) *10 Mindful Minutes: Giving Our Children - and Ourselves – the Social and Emotional Skills to Reduce Stress and Anxiety for Healthier, Happier Lives.* PIATKUS BOOKS.
  www.thehawnfoundation.org

- © 2011 Lauren Alderfer, text, and Kerry Lee MacLean, illustrations, *Mindful Monkey, Happy Panda*. Reprinted by arrangement with WISDOM PUBLICATIONS, INC., WISDOMPUBS.ORG.
- Willard, Christopher. (2011) *"Child's Mind – Mindfulness Practices to help our children be more focused calm and relaxed."* PARALLAX PRESS.

   www.drchristopherwillard.com

Programs
Katsikis, Sandra , (2013) Stretch and Connect program
www.soothingsouls.com.au

13 – CALM CHILDREN
Reading
- Murray , Lorraine E . (2012) *Calm Kids – Help children relax with mindful activities.* FLORIS BOOKS   www.teachchildrenmeditation.com
- *Relax Kids – The wishing star 52 meditations for children (aged 5+)* Marneta Viegas. Illustrations by Nicola Wyldbore-Smith
- www.dalailama.com

14 – YOUR CHILD IS YOUR GURU
Reading
- Lindsell, Fenella, Y*ogaBugs - The one bug kids should catch*, VIRGIN BOOKS, 2008

Teacher training courses
YogaBugs - www.yogabugs.com.au
Radiant Child - www.childrensyoga.com
Rainbow Kids - www.rainbowkidsyoga.net

15 - BE THE LIGHTHOUSE
Training
Kundalini Womens Camp in Australia 2013.
Anastasia Williams   www.anastasia-williams.com

Reading
- Khalsa, Shakta Kaur (2000) *Kundalini Yoga – Unlock your inner potential through life changing exercise.* DK PUBLISHING.
www.3ho.org
www.brenebrown.com

RESOURCES

Music
www.buddharadio.com.au
www.snatamkaur.com
www.rootlight.com

Recommended reading for you
- Dugan, Jan, Gudkovs, Jan. (2012) *The focused child – How yoga can help you raise healthy, contented children. Focus Child Trust.*
- Kabat-Zinn , Jon, Kabat-Zinn, Myla. (1997) *Everyday Blessings – The Inner Work of Mindful Parenting.* HYPERION BOOKS.
- Griffiths, Andrew, (2009) *"The Me Myth. What do you mean it's not all about me?* SIMON AND SCHUSTER.   www.andrewgriffiths.com.au
- Dr. Laura Markham *Peaceful Parenting*   www.ahaparenting.com

Recommended reading for your children
- Hay, Louise L. (2008) Schwarz, Manuela, Illustrations. *"I think I am – teaching kids the power of affirmations."* HAY HOUSE.
- Dyer, Wayne W., Siegel, Melanie, illustrations. (2005) *Incredible You. 10 ways to let your greatness shine through.* HAY HOUSE.
- Dyer, Wayne W. Budnick, Stacy Heller, Illustrations. (2006) *Unstoppable Me. 10 ways to soar through life.* HAY HOUSE.
- MacLean, Kerry Lee. (2004) *"Peaceful Piggy Meditation".*
- MacLean, Kerry Lee. (2009) *"Moody Cow Meditates".* www.kerryleemacleanauthor.com
- Nagaraja, Dharmachari, (2008) *"Buddha at Bedtime – Tales of love and wisdom for you to read with your child to enchant, enlighten and inspire.* WATKINS PUBLISHING.

Mother Om Loves ....
www.motherzen.com
www.betterbeginnings.com.au
www.pinkymckay.com
www.bellybelly.com.au

From our Yoga Mamata families...

Kids' yoga

My eldest daughter started yoga with Mamata when she was three. It quickly became the highlight of her week. The classes were always captivating and full of adventure whether it was an African jungle safari or underwater mermaid escapade. My daughter not only enjoyed the classes but loved practising at home what she had learnt. She would regularly do her sun salutations either on her own or with me during my yoga practice and often used her mind jar and yoga breathing to calm herself down when she was upset. My daughter is now four and my youngest (two-and-a-half year old) has also joined the class and I can see the amazing benefits continuing with both of them.

Taryn, Mother. BApp. Sc.

Mum and baby yoga

I started Leonie's mum and baby yoga class when my son Tasman was about two months old. Leonie's class helped me to be more calm and present in the challenging early months of being a new mum. Tasman and I both loved that time together, away from the distractions of chores and housework, as well as the interaction with other mums and bubs. Physically, it also really helped me get back into shape after pregnancy.

Ruth, Mother.

Family yoga

Leonie's family yoga classes are a real treat- a rare chance to connect spiritually with your partner and children while having fun and a good stretch! I particularly love the family poses we have learnt as they are a fun way to reconnect at home. Leonie teaches yoga from the heart and incorporates mindful techniques with fun drama games to keep the kids interested.

Majella, Mother.

Mamata retreats

I can highly recommend Leonie's retreat. Leonie herself radiates a warmth and positive energy that is infectious. She is a wealth of valuable knowledge around wellbeing and mindfulness especially when it comes to daily interactions with your kids. You will learn lessons on this retreat that you will use forever. The other amazing benefits were a breathtaking setting, delicious, healthy, nutritious food with recipes to take home, great yoga and a host of meditations. You will come away feeling truly amazing. Every mum needs to jump on this.
Bridget, Mother.

Child care

When Leonie first approached me with the idea of YogaBugs for our childcare centre, I didn't need to think twice. I was very impressed with Leonie's attitude to life, to children and their mothers, and the whole concept of yoga and meditation. We have had weekly yoga classes since then. The children, from the youngest child to the eldest, enjoy them and benefit from them immensely.
Sandra Bell, Director, Randwick Open Care for Kids

Connect with Mamata

www.yogamamata.com

www.facebook.com/yogamamata

Twitter @yogamamata

Instagram yogamamata

ACKNOWLEDGMENTS

Writing this book has been an overwhelming, beautiful, cathartic, intense and rewarding experience.

I feel like I have created and birthed another baby. I am filled with awe and love for how this has changed my life.

These words would not have been written if my son's father and I had not decided to end our marriage. A broken heart is the ultimate teacher and although this situation still fills my heart with sadness, I am so grateful it happened. I found my light and now have the joy of sharing my journey and healing others.

Thank you to the KPI crew and my GSD group. It is inspiring to be surrounded with greatness and others who have already walked this path of being an author, keeping me focused and motivated.

It takes a team of talented people to write a book. Thank you to my editor Lucy, for turning my words into a flowing manuscript that represents the essence of feeling calm, connected and content.

Thank you to my designer Pauline for the beautiful layout and for being patient with the process. Thanks also to my father who, as a grammatical guru has helped me immensely. I love you Dad.

Whilst writing this book, a beautiful man called Jarkko wandered into my life and we all fell in love as a family. Jarkko, his dog Edi, Lael and I are creating a life together as a rainbow family and I thank the universe every day for this cosmic connection.

I have dedicated this book to my family, my yoga practice and my son, Lael. I would not have completed this process without their guidance, love and support.

Thank you Lael for teaching me how to be the best version of myself; reminding me to 'unplug and play' and to see that happiness is right now in this moment.

Thank you to all the families, mothers and children that have supported my business and are passionate about my vision to open a café style studio dedicated to yoga and family.

The divine light in me salutes the divine light within you.
Namaste

Printed in Great Britain
by Amazon